Beyond the Power of Love

Beyond the Power of Love

A Woman's Journey through Betrayal
of Religion and Spousal Abuse

Janice Romney

iUniverse, Inc.
Bloomington

Beyond the Power of Love
A Woman's Journey through Betrayal of
Religion and Spousal Abuse

iUniverse books may be ordered through booksellers or by contacting:

iUniverse
1663 Liberty Drive
Bloomington, IN 47403
www.iuniverse.com
1-800-Authors (1-800-288-4677)

Because of the dynamic nature of the Internet, any web addresses or links contained in this book may have changed since publication and may no longer be valid. The views expressed in this work are solely those of the author and do not necessarily reflect the views of the publisher, and the publisher hereby disclaims any responsibility for them.

Any people depicted in stock imagery provided by Thinkstock are models, and such images are being used for illustrative purposes only.

Certain stock imagery © Thinkstock.

ISBN: 978-1-4759-5927-7 (sc)
ISBN: 978-1-4759-5928-4 (hc)
ISBN: 978-1-4759-5929-1 (e)

Library of Congress Control Number: 2012920797

Printed in the United States of America

iUniverse rev. date: 10/29/2012

With my deepest love, I dedicate this story to the one who has carried me through the storms of life, whose love was given in abundance and unconditionally. Without you, Mom, my children and I would not have the life we live today; words cannot describe the love and gratitude I feel for you in my heart. I have been blessed through the grace of God.

Contents

Preface

Beyond the Power of Love: A Woman's Journey through Betrayal of Religion and Spousal Abuse is a revision of *Beneath Wings of an Angel*, which was first published in 2004. This book reveals the different forms of abuse, the effects, and how we attract relationships that mirror our beliefs about ourselves. Often change is difficult, and at times we become trapped in fear, unable to make important decisions that affect us and also others. Ending the cycle of abuse takes the help of many, but the most important things are prevention, education, intervention and the healing that comes from the power of love.

This is why I want to publish this book again and write about my experiences as a mother and a woman who has lived through abuse, divorce, marriage, transformation, and fallen dreams, yet knows the healing power of love. As I began moving forward out of darkness and toward light in my life, I also faced the pain and anger of my children and what it did to their lives. With this dark storm, I faced more guilt and sorrow reliving a life I thought we had left behind.

But on this path, a granddaughter was born. Her little heart is filled with God's love. As if destiny gifted her to us, she is a source of healing my family needed to draw us together and be renewed by her love.

During a difficult period of time, I also faced my own chilling winter without spring, and fifteen years later, I was divorced once again. Like a caterpillar, I wove a cocoon to shield myself from what I felt was the death of my soul—perhaps my own metamorphosis. Inside this cocoon, my path took me to the depths of personal hell, the edge of life, and the deepest aspect of my heart. With each trial, I sought the comfort of the light within, and when I couldn't see, I learned to trust my inner voice. When I was at my lowest point, when I had no will to go on, my authentic voice challenged me with my greatest test. Had I not learned self-trust, I would not have life today. Had I stayed in my home in Mexico and not left when told to leave, I would not have been close enough to a hospital when, the following morning, I came close to death with a near-fatal brain tumor.

Throughout our trials, God has blessed us with the greatest gift of all, the enlightenment of the divine spark of life, the melody of heaven, which is the power of His love. This eternal love reaches into the very darkest corners of human hearts, and love is the light that fills every little cell and fiber of our being, a pure love that is felt in every tissue of the heart. How can we not be changed within ourselves as we learn to forgive, understand, and have compassion for our own imperfections? As we are changed from within, we learn to trust our authentic voice and the guidance we receive. With this light we become love; we then send forth this vibration into the universe, the melody of love to heal the earth and all of humanity.

October 14, 2012

Dearest Mom:

Words spoken could not do you justice in expressing how the unrelenting immensity of your heart has changed my life and that of countless many. I decided to write you because you've inspired me to do so. How good it feels to be inspired. It's a feeling that most will never have the opportunity to experience such as I have had being your son and under your foster all my life. I cannot imagine the pain and hardships you have endured, but with the passion that is expressed in your writing, I can feel the love with which you overcame it all. It really makes me proud to be your son.

In a lot of ways, I am honored to have had the opportunity to experience what you have given me. When I said you have prepared a paradise for generations to come, it is because your love is so profoundly strong it will permeate with a brilliant pervasiveness throughout all time. Sometimes our faith falters like flailing peddles of a sun-starved flower, but with direction and focus, the light can renew and strengthen us enough to bear the emanation of our beauty. Like a sun-flower turning its face with the rise and fall of the sun, so shall we remain always to let the light illuminate our inner brilliance. For it is in effort that light or faith is obtained, an everlasting hope carrying us on as we sleep through the night. You are my sunshine.

You've been a forge of my intellectual love, mom. And being able to but in part understand true love like you do, is like sitting with the angels on high. Mom, you will always be my Angel.

I love you with all of my heart.

Westin

A Personal Note from the Author

When I first began writing 2004, it was for my personal healing and a desire to find wholeness and truth. How could I have known the changes it would take to heal and reveal the authentic voice, the radiant light within me? It has been a long journey, especially for the healing of my children. Today, my voice retraces my steps as a young child, woman, wife, and mother to bring you to the current changes existing in our lives. My hope is that you will think about your own life and not wait for the years to force you away from pain to find love, wholeness and deep, inner peace.

With love and blessings,

Janice

1

Childhood Memories of Abuse

I did not lose myself all at once. I rubbed out my face over the years
washing away my pain, the same way carvings
on stone are worn down by water.
—Amy Tan

In faded, misty memories, I'm five years old again. I can still see the bright red lipstick marks on my bottom as I tried to wash them away, and I remember the look on my mother's face when she unexpectedly opened the bathroom door and caught me. "What are you doing?" she said. "What is all over your bottom?" I don't remember how I answered her; I just remember her look and the guilt I felt when she said, "Shame on you," but I know she didn't know the truth.

That afternoon, the child so filled with grace simply slipped away. My face no longer bore the rays of sunlight. Instead, guilt colored my world in hues of amber gray. Over the years, the memory of childhood sexual abuse was embedded so deeply, I had virtually forgotten. Purged from my conscious mind was the memory of an older adult male who, while I was playing away from home, took me

1

into his bathroom and made me stand on top of the toilet seat, with my back facing him. He laughed as he made fun of me, humiliating me unmercifully and making me feel small and helpless.

He didn't listen when I said, "No, I don't want to." He didn't care as my sobbing washed away my plea, "Just let me go home." I still remember the words he said: "I'm not going to hurt you, just take off your clothes." I distinctly remember bright red lipstick from a makeup kit on the bathroom counter. He told me to use the lipstick, and I obeyed. Opening the tube, I painted my lips just before he placed his hands and fingers on my bottom.

Helplessly frightened, I begged him to stop, but he didn't listen. He took the lipstick away from me. Playfully, he touched my bottom with it and asked me how it felt. Tightly closing my eyes and holding my breath, I held back tears. The most haunting memory of all was the moment he forced himself inside me. As I braced myself against the mirror, my little knees were trembling; pain seared through me, and even though I wanted to scream, the words just wouldn't come. They felt frozen and trapped inside. Yet to myself I swore, *I hate him, I hate him.*

When he was finished, he said, "Time for you to go home," just as he closed the door behind him. After pulling on my clothes, I timidly opened the door and found him waiting on the other side. "You were the one who asked for this. If you tell anyone, you'll be punished, so this had better be our little secret."

Humiliated, I walked home along the dusty country road, staring at my shoes and fighting back the tears. Gently I whispered, *"Don't cry; after all, it wasn't your fault"*. Time and again I tried to reassure myself, *"You said no; he just wouldn't listen. But what about my bottom?"* I didn't want to go home. I felt guilty and ashamed of myself. *"I know my mom will see, what will she say? What will she think of me?"*

Today, I still see the face of this little girl and still remember how I walked toward home a little slower than I did before I went out to play, wiping each tear away as it stained my freckled face. Somehow I knew I would have to hide my secret and never tell a soul. I was dirty now—not from playing hide-and-seek, but from letting someone touch me in places that evoked deep, deep inner shame.

As years went by, my memory of the abuse completely vanished. By the time I entered high school, cheerleading, acting in plays, proms, riding my horse along the river, and falling desperately in love were as much a part of growing up as my deepest feelings of shame.

Each lesson in my young women's class at church only solidified that I was unclean without my knowing why. I was afraid to be loved and yet more afraid that I wasn't. My boundaries had been destroyed, and yet I was taught to be morally clean so that I would be a choice spirit of my Heavenly Father. As the years went by, I lost all touch with those buried feelings, and I pulled further away from the delightful child that I must have been.

Even today, I can distantly see myself as a child with a happy face, but my heart reaches out to that girl as I feel her loneliness. I feel compassion for the extreme sensitivity she once felt and her need to hear a word of praise.

I was just nineteen years old when my father, only forty-eight, died of a sudden heart attack. Nothing remained the same after his death, especially the life of a make-believe princess I had created for myself. Looking back, it could have been that I suffered from depression from a very early age and at this point it worsened—but in any event, I went untreated and continued to spiral ever downward.

I kept a diary for many years, and one day I opened my book and began to read. My writing startled me—the unhappiness, loss of direction, loneliness, and desperation flowed through the ink and onto the pages. Repeatedly I wrote, "If I just stay obedient, God will bless me."

Years later, I could not find the stability I longed for. I was unhappy and lived in the past. In time, my anger turned me against God. The only thing that kept me going was the belief that if I could just find someone to love me, my life would be different.

I studied for a while in Utah. My hope was to become an elementary-school teacher, but that soon changed, so I moved to Phoenix in 1975. I rented a one-bedroom house close to my work. I loved the warmth of the sun and the smell of orange blossoms, and in time, my spirits were lifted and I felt hopeful. For the first time, I was experiencing myself in a way that gave me a sense of freedom. I was going to live my life without expecting God to bless me or punish me, and I no longer felt that I had to be married.

I found clerical work in a home for unwed mothers and actually enjoyed the work I was doing. My eyes opened to a whole different world, one that wasn't pristine and perfect from the outside. This world included young girls pregnant from rape or incest and the people trying to help them. Most of the girls were only fourteen years old, and yet they were young mothers just trying to finish high school and cope with their emotional trauma.

One afternoon, I returned home from work to find my apartment had been vandalized. A police officer responded to my call, but it was obvious he was more interested in me than in filling out his report. He was blond with incredible blue eyes and skin beautifully bronzed by the Arizona sun. I was as attracted to him as he was to me, and I was extremely flattered when he invited me to a party given by one of the officers that he worked with. I wasn't the least bit concerned that I didn't really know him. He was a police officer. I couldn't be any safer—or so I believed.

He picked me up Friday night after work, and we drove across Phoenix to his friend's condo. The party was crowded with people drinking alcohol and having a great time. I was uncomfortable because I didn't drink. Stan brought me a soft drink instead, but it wasn't long before I felt light-headed and wanted to lie down. He offered to take me upstairs, but I insisted on going home. We drove back to my place, and since I still felt dizzy, he carried me into my bedroom and placed me on my bed. He began undressing me, and I tried to stop him. Grabbing hold of my arms, he pinned them above my head and aggressively started kissing me. He was rough and made my lips bleed. I was terrified!

I struggled against his brutal force when he violently began ripping off my clothing. His body weight was suffocating, and I was petrified, screaming at the same time, "Stop, you're hurting me." He put his hand over my mouth, and the next thing I remember were early morning rays of sun filtering through my bedroom window.

As I awoke, I touched my body, and in my nakedness froze for just a moment. I hurt and my body ached. My heart raced and my thoughts ran wild. What had happened last night? My head was foggy, and I could only remember bits and pieces of the night before. Nothing made sense, and when reality finally hit me like a ton of bricks, I realized I had been raped.

What had I ever done to deserve this? Hot water flowing into my bathtub rinsed my body clean, but it didn't take away the physical pain or remove the inner filth that seemed to be a part of me. Still shocked and confused, I realized how naïve I had been.

Just the night before, I had left home with a wonderful date, feeling all grown-up and ready to take on the world, but this morning I woke up defiled and shattered not only as a woman, but also in my faith.

Finally, I confided in Karen, a friend at work, and she had to explain things I didn't understand. She told me about date rape. Karen explained about a drug given to rape victims so they don't remember what happened. In my naïveté, I was startled. I had never heard of anything like that before. Karen, years younger than I, had grown up in a world much different from mine. The excruciating pain I felt for days confused me, but Karen didn't hesitate to say, "You've also been sodomized."

Karen helped me go through the process of filing rape charges against the officer, but that wasn't successful because all of his buddies at work gave him alibis and said they had never seen me. I was shocked when I received word that the county attorney's office would not file charges against the officer. Because I bathed and didn't report the rape for several days, I was without the physical evidence needed, and I had no choice but to drop the charges and get on with my life. I vowed never to allow myself the humiliation, embarrassment, and utter frustration of being a victim all over again. Growing up in a small country community hadn't prepared me for this, even though I don't think anyone is prepared regardless of her background. The legal system can be brutally unjust to victims.

Nothing I did ended with a positive result. Then I told myself, *"Just put it away, Janice, like a game you no longer want to play. Pretend it doesn't matter, and it will go away."*

Two months later, I realized I was pregnant. The emotional trauma from that terrifying night and the helplessness I felt caused extreme turmoil, and I felt more alone than I had ever felt before. Afraid of facing the ugliness in me, my only thought was, *"How can I tell my mother?"* The reason for my pregnancy didn't seem to matter. I felt dirty and that I was somehow to blame. I never met my date before and never saw him after that night, but he changed my life forever.

Nighttime offered little relief, and often I would awaken screaming without being able to make a sound. Paralyzed with fear, I soon realized my nightmares had more to do with my past. Perhaps the present emotional trauma triggered abandoned and long-forgotten memories as they sprang forth rapidly; growing like tiny tangled vines that consumed all light. Shame, the one feeling I had hidden since I was a child, was staring me in the face.

I didn't remember everything, yet I still knew that as a child I had been deeply hurt. I remembered being in a bathroom with a tube of bright red lipstick, but when I felt hands and fingers touching me, I desperately wanted the memory to stop. Grabbing at hands that were no longer there felt repulsive. Feelings of sexual stimulation sent me into a spiraling spin of shame, and in vain I cried, "Please, God, just make this stop." Feelings of guilt carried me to a frightening place where I didn't want to be.

I tried getting in touch with the bishop of the ward I was in, but he never returned my calls. I was not permitted to talk about personal matters with the counselors at work, and yet I tried many times to reach one who I admired later in the evening at her home. She had a small family and put me off enough times that I stopped calling her. Without knowing where else to turn, I looked in the Yellow Pages. I found a number under Planned Parenthood, so I called and made an appointment. At first I felt relieved, believing I would find the support I needed.

My appointment was in the evening after work. First I had to take a pregnancy test. Several days later, when the test results were finished, I had another appointment. The woman I saw didn't see my situation as a sinful one, but rather one that I could change. Stunned, I sat quite still in my chair as she talked about alternative solutions.

"Why are you so afraid?" she asked.

"Don't you offer unwed mothers help, such as prenatal care or adoption?" I answered.

Unfortunately, the only solution Planned Parenthood had was to terminate the pregnancy. "It wasn't a baby," the woman said, "just an undeveloped fetus without any feeling." I felt life drain out of me as panic set in. In a heartbeat, my life had completely changed, and yet even today I can hear her say, "You don't have to carry a pregnancy that is a result of rape."

After leaving Planned Parenthood, I went home and thought about the only solution I had been offered. During the following days, I functioned as if in a fog. Nothing seemed real. Over and over I thought about the night I was raped. I wanted to remember so that I could absolve myself of guilt.

I had already been given a referral to a doctor who would perform the procedure, and I knew the choice I had made was the only choice I had. Within a few days, I scheduled an appointment with this doctor. His office was just like any other—I could even pretend I was there for a routine checkup. As the doctor explained the procedure, I closed my eyes and tried to fight back the tears, but they flowed from such a deep place inside me that I couldn't stop them.

During the '70s, abortion was a two-day procedure. The first day, they inserted something to make me dilate. Later that night, I felt mild contractions. In agony, I lay awake, sobs wracking my body, and I felt emotionally exhausted before sunrise. Even if I wanted to change my mind, it was too late. I had all night to feel the torment of my most difficult choice. I mourned the coming death of my baby as anguish tore at my soul. My only thoughts were that now God must surely be angry with me; I had finally given Him reason to punish me, and I felt sure my soul was damned.

The following morning, I was wheeled into a room I remember very little about. The operating room was cold and sterile. Lights showered the room with an eerie brightness, and all I could see were people with gloves dressed in white saying, "It will be over soon."

Several weeks later, I went home to visit my mother, and there was a "fireside" held at the chapel that night. I was sitting in the front pew when the lights went out and the movie started. Soft music began to play, and immediately I knew what the film was about. I wanted to run, but I knew I couldn't. Instead, I slithered into my seat, closing my eyes, wanting to be anywhere else but there. Excruciating guilt welled up inside, and I knew that I had to leave as

I fought back tears. Darkness closed in on me as if I were about to suffocate. I felt lights surrounding me, with every eye watching. Of course, no one else knew what I was going through, but I felt this film was just for me. Right in front of me was a screen that appeared enormous. A young pregnant girl was seeking guidance; abortion was a choice she had been given. As the film progressed, the message given was that abortion is a sin akin to murder. The message was clear: "Taking the life of an unborn child is a heinous sin and one that you may *never* be forgiven for."

Each spoken word flowed through me like a cold winter's chill. The words "heinous sin" played over and over like a broken phonograph record inside my head.

Calmly I rose from my seat. Methodically I walked to the door as if nothing was wrong. My heart was pounding and my legs felt weak as I desperately tried to keep myself from screaming. Tears had already soaked my face by the time I walked through the chapel doors, and I hung my head in shame wanting to die if for no other reason than to rid myself of the pain.

Fighting the cold night air, I walked home desperately trying to erase the images from my mind. I didn't even have to close my eyes to see the fetus recoil in its attempt to survive; this little clump of cells felt the pain inflicted by the instruments used to destroy its life.

The film showed the fetus as it was developing through each phase. During the abortion procedure, limbs were literally ripped from the body as the fetus was torn from the womb. I felt nauseated and emotionally traumatized by what I saw. That little lump of cells was actually a baby with fingers, toes, legs, and arms, and I could even see the heart beat.

From that day on, I knew I could never be forgiven, and subconsciously I went out of my way to find those who would punish me. Because something inside of me had died with the abortion,

I became someone I didn't even recognize. Everything about me changed, including my values.

Within a few months, I moved away from my little one-bedroom house in Phoenix, yearning to forget about my past and start my life over. I found a new job at a law firm and moved into an apartment in Mesa, Arizona. Fate was starting another chapter in my life, but once again it was being written with unresolved heartache and secrets from my past. I did what I had always done, buried my deepest feelings and started over.

I became promiscuous. I looked for and found men to date who would hurt me. After work I would stop at a nightclub, and I would always find someone to flirt with. This was a new me—flirtatious without any intention of saying no when the guy asked to take me home, knowing exactly what he wanted. Today I cringe at my scandalous behavior, and even though I felt used by the men I was with, perhaps what I didn't realize at the time was that I was only using them in transferring the pain I felt.

When I was young, I couldn't understand why God was punishing me, but on the day of the abortion I became someone who deserved to be punished and abandoned by a God who, I had been taught, would not tolerate the least degree of sin. This traumatic procedure was a never-ending nightmare of anguish. I grieved in a way that I never got over, and my life was never the same. But this little secret was placed somewhere deep inside along with my unfinished grieving for my father, my failures, and my buried memories of childhood sexual abuse.

2

Trapped Inside an
Abusive Relationship

*Love is symbolic of warmth and friendship. Love is also
being who you are and allowing others to be who they are
without forcing change, but never should love hurt.*

It was a Sunday afternoon, and I was sitting in Sunday worship across the aisle from a man who kept drawing my attention. As our eyes met, I felt our mutual attraction, but it made me uneasy. It was as though an inner voice was whispering, *"You know him, but stay away from him"*.

Bobby and I lived in the same apartment complex, and after seeing him in church, I met him later again that week by the pool. That uneasy feeling didn't leave me, but something about the way he talked to me as he said, "When I first saw you, I saw the sadness in your eyes," made me think twice about my feelings. I was ready to throw caution to the wind. He seemed so caring.

We were both raised in devout Mormon families, and even though he had been inactive, he seemed to have turned his life around. Recently divorced, he was going to church every Sunday, paying his tithes, and obeying the Word of Wisdom. More than anything, he wanted to be married in the temple.

In the weeks that followed, we spent quite a bit of time together. One evening, we had gone out to dinner, and the waiter spilled water on me. As the waiter mumbled an apology, he quickly tried to clean up the mess he made. Even though my dress was wet, I laughed and told him not to worry about it, but Bobby didn't think it was funny and told him so.

"You're a damn fool," he said. With that insult, the waiter was clearly embarrassed, and frankly, I was shocked by Bobby's rudeness.

When we got to the car, I sat close to him. Once we were ready to leave, he put the car into drive when he should have put it in reverse and drove over a cement block. The car rocked back and forth until all four wheels rested on the ground. I laughed because it seemed so funny, but he didn't laugh. Instead, he was angry with me. He said I tried to humiliate him. When I innocently said he was being silly, a darker side of him emerged.

Abruptly, he turned and shouted in my face that I was laughing at him.

Jolted by his reaction, I defended myself. "I wasn't laughing at you."

"Like hell you weren't. Do you think you're better than me?"

Shocked more than anything, I moved away from him, and then he leaned over just far enough into my face to scare me.

He drove to our apartment complex, stopped the car, and said nothing. I half expected him to walk me to my door but felt relieved when he didn't.

Bobby called me the following day at work to say he was sorry, but I wasn't interested in an apology, I didn't want to see him again, but at noon he came by the office with flowers in hand. He spent the next hour, over lunch, telling me how sorry he was for the way he behaved. Tearfully, he justified his behavior as he said, "I was completely out of line, I had a bad day at work, and I'm sorry I took it out on you." He also explained that every woman he had ever been with had betrayed him, and he was afraid I would do the same. By the time he drove me back to the office, all was forgiven.

There were two sides to Bobby, and he kept me guessing as to which one would show up when we were together. At times he was easy to be with, but in a heartbeat he could change, and I always felt on edge. Still, I continued to see him.

Several months later, he asked me to marry him. At first I didn't have an answer. There was a part of me that wanted to say yes and another part that didn't.

The night air was cool, and I felt pressured into saying yes. Finally I gave in. He was also insistent that we shouldn't wait. Suddenly, I felt nervous. Perhaps it was the night air, or maybe the urgency with which he spoke of our wedding date that sent a chill through me. I didn't want to rush into marriage, but Bobby was in a hurry. How I felt didn't matter.

After we had been engaged for a few weeks, I knew I needed to share my secret with him. Maybe I just needed to absolve my soul. My secret weighed heavily upon me, and I had been taught that there was only one way to be forgiven and that was through confession. Bobby demanded absolute honesty from me, and I believed that if I opened up and came clean, he would learn to trust me.

Carefully, without telling him why, I explained that I needed to see our bishop before we could set a wedding date. Suspicious, he wanted to know why, but I wasn't ready to tell him.

After making an appointment, I went to see my bishop. Knowing the reason for my appointment, the bishop had arranged our meeting to be that of an official church court, which meant I would meet with not only the bishop but also his first and second counselors.

I really didn't know what to expect, but sitting before God's adjudicators on the eve of my judgment only reinforced my need to be punished. Three chairs were placed next to each other at the front of the room, with one single chair placed in the middle facing the other three. The bishop and his two counselors took their seats and told me to take mine. As I looked into the penetrating eyes of my bishop—to me, an almighty force—I felt myself disintegrate into a disgraceful little girl. It seemed to take forever for the words to come. At first I didn't know where to start, but once I did, I poured my heart out. I wept, as they remained silent. I waited for their response.

My bishop was more compassionate, but one of his counselors couldn't quite conceive of any woman doing what I had done— aborting my child. I could see it in his facial expressions, and when I described certain details, his eyes grew wide. He raised his eyebrows so high; they nearly flew off his face. Then he wanted more intimate details.

Even though I explained that my pregnancy was a result of date rape, he kept repeating the same question, "But you agreed to go out with this guy, didn't you?" and "After you went to his place, you invited him into your apartment, didn't you?" and "Are you sure you didn't drink that night or act in any way that would lead him on?"

Humiliated beyond words, I felt like he was insinuating I couldn't be raped if I invited him into my home.

I felt the tears would never stop as I waited outside the office while the three men who held my fate in their hands made a decision. The events of the church court replayed in my mind, and I felt confused.

Once they had agreed upon their decision, I was summoned into the bishop's office. That night, disciplinary action was taken against me. It was the decision of the court that I was to be disfellowshipped, which meant that my name would still remain on church records but I would be forbidden to partake of the sacrament or participate in church callings for six months.

Even though I accepted their decision that night, I felt shunned, and the most devastating thing I felt was that in God's eyes I was still a sinner until I could atone or feel sufficient sorrow to pay the price for my sins. As I walked away that night, I realized just how well-acquainted I had become with sorrow, and how feelings of unworthiness had walked every step of the way with me since I was a child.

I left the bishop's office and drove home. I parked outside my apartment, but instead of going home, I walked the short distance to Bobby's. I knew he would be waiting to hear from me. As soon as I neared his door, a feeling of caution came over me. The moment I raised my hand to knock on his door, I quickly turned away, but before I had the chance to run, the door opened and Bobby was staring me in the face. His eyes were stone cold, and I knew he was angry. Harshly, he told me to come in. That was the last thing I wanted to do, so I said it was late, and I would talk to him the following day.

He grabbed me by the arm and jerked me inside. Frightened, I told him to get his hands off me, but instead he threw me across the room, locking the deadbolt to the door behind him. Then he forced me to sit down. Standing over me, Bobby demanded to know exactly why I went to see the bishop.

My heart raced. My instinctive reaction was to say something that would calm him down, so I lied when I answered him, "The bishop was busy and we never got a chance to meet."

He jumped in my face, grabbing me by the shoulders, shaking me. "You're lying," he yelled. "I saw your car over there for more than two hours."

Pushing him away, I answered, "This is insane, Bobby, and I don't even know what you want from me." By this time I was really frightened.

"You know exactly what I want," he shouted.

Terrified, I begged, "Please don't do this, Bobby! I can't talk to you when you are like this."

He had me pinned against my chair. I felt threatened, interrogated, and humiliated. I also tried in vain to convince him I hadn't spoken with the bishop.

Back and forth he paced, stopping only to get in my face. "You'll pay for this," he shouted.

He grabbed my shoulders and shook me violently, demanding an answer. With his face in mine, I had no other choice; I had to tell him that I had been disfellowshipped. "Just back off, Bobby, and I'll tell you why."

I don't know if I was more frightened or angry. He held me against my will and forced me to share my deepest hurt with him, a raging maniac, when he really didn't care how I felt.

Bobby moved far enough away, and then I told him. "I can't marry you in the temple, Bobby, at least not for six months."

Swiftly, he lunged at me. I ducked, and his fist barely missed my face as his hand slammed into the couch behind me. Hurling insults, he wanted me to know how cheap and disgusting I was.

What a fool I must have been. An hour had passed since I'd first knocked on Bobby's door, and he already knew what took place at the bishop's office that evening.

"I've never trusted you from the beginning," he said. "I knew you were a liar underneath that perfect little rich girl you pretend to be. Tonight you've proven who you really are."

He waved his arms self-righteously and shook his fists at me as he explained that for the first time, I was being forced to see myself as I really was. It was his duty, he said, to follow me that afternoon when I met with the bishop. Then he quietly listened behind closed doors to every word spoken.

Feeling betrayed and humiliated, I tried to stand up. I was

through listening to him, and I was angry. Instantly reacting, he grabbed me and shoved me against the chair. "You're not getting out of here!" he yelled. He was hurtling insults and demanding answers from me, but he wouldn't even let me speak.

"You lied to me," he yelled repeatedly. "I thought you were decent but you're not."

At a loss for anything to say, I begged him to stop yelling at me. What I said only added fuel to the fire.

Grabbing me by the hair, he dragged me from the couch and threw me to the floor. "How can you ever make this up to me?" he hollered with his face in mine.

Kicking and screaming, I struggled against him as he bashed my head against the floor. Paralyzed with fear, I felt my mind spinning, but no matter what I said, he would mock me unmercifully. "Please don't hurt me," he would sneer in my face. "Poor little girl! What's the matter? You afraid of me?"

Pinning my hands above my head, he held me down, laughing because I begged him to let me go. But all too soon, his laughter turned chilling.

With his face inches from mine, he said I deserved to be punished for killing an unborn baby. He said I deserved to be punished for whoring around and cheating him out of a temple marriage. He threatened to tell my sisters about my abortion—he wanted to make sure everyone knew that it was I who was guilty of immorality.

All the emotions pent up inside me exploded. I was hurting, but not from Bobby physically restraining me or bashing my head against the floor. Everything he said about me was true. My head was spinning, and I felt nauseated. I saw the same repulsive reaction earlier that night in the bishop's office. With tears streaming down my face, I wept.

Slowly, Bobby lessened his grip on me.

"Go to hell, Bobby," I said.

In disgust, Bobby lifted his body off mine and moved away from me. For a second, I thought I had a chance. I tried to get up and run for the door, but he grabbed me and knocked me to the floor, raging, "Where in the hell do you think you're going?"

As I screamed for help, he clamped his hand over my mouth, and then, instantly, with both hands he reached around my neck, trying to choke the life out of me. Gasping for air, I struggled. Wildly thrashing, I thought I was going to die. Loud pounding on the door stopped him as a neighbor yelled, "Is everything all right in there?"

Bobby let go of me and then hollered, "Nothing is wrong, so mind your own damn business." The neighbor walked away, but Bobby also let me up from the floor.

As soon as he moved far enough away from the door, I made a break for it. With my heart pounding, I fumbled to unlock the deadbolt, and then I grabbed the doorknob. The second it opened, I was out of there. Terrified, I made my way back to my apartment and immediately locked the door behind me, unable to believe I was finally home.

The following day, a florist dropped off a bouquet of flowers with a note saying how sorry he was for what happened the night before. Several days later, he called me at work and asked if we could meet for lunch, and I refused. Later on during that week, I was working late, and although the doors were locked to the office building there was a large window in front of my desk. I looked up and saw Bobby standing in front of the window. Startled, I motioned to him to leave me alone. He stood there for some time and then left.

The weekend passed without my seeing him. I stayed close by a friend and ignored him, but as soon as I went to work on Monday, another bouquet of flowers arrived. Bobby was not going to leave me alone. Finally, I agreed to meet with him.

He wanted me to know all about him and why it was so hard

for him to trust me, and why a temple marriage was so important to him. He went on to tell me that his mother died when he was four. He lived with relatives who sexually and physically abused him. Later on, his father remarried, but that didn't end the abuse in his life. To escape a stepmother he detested, he ran away from home at the age of fourteen. Later, he joined the navy, eventually becoming a Navy Seal during the Vietnam War.

Seeing tears fill his eyes, I believed he had a heart. I gently held his hand, telling him how sorry I was for the life he had lived. At that moment, I believed I could make things up to him.

Springtime is one of the loveliest times in Arizona, and I soaked in the attention he showered on me along with the sun. My heart, parched and withered from betrayal, felt nourished in the warmth of romance and a sense of belonging. Seeing this other side to him, I believed that all I had to do was nurture this side and he would change.

We spent a few days in the White Mountains sightseeing and hiking. One morning, I looked in the mirror, and the reflection I saw revealed a glow that hadn't been there before. Later on, Bobby took a photo of me standing beneath a tall pine tree.

One candid photograph, which I held on to for many years revealed something lost and forgotten—a beautiful young woman still clinging to her hopes and dreams.

Once I was away from the cool mountain air, the valley brought me back to reality. No matter how hard I tried to love Bobby, I only brought out his anger, and he never let me forget it. Because of his volatile temper, I broke off our engagement several times, but he would come back begging my forgiveness. In tears, once again, he would recall memories of childhood abuse and how hard it was for him to trust. He swore that he was willing to work on it. In time, this became the only part of his heart he entrusted to me; in fact, it was our only means of bonding, one wounded heart to another.

Every night after work, we walked around the temple grounds, a favorite place of ours, and planned our future. Beneath the starlit sky, Bobby said I was the woman who would change his life. Holding hands as we walked through fragrant gardens filled with blooming flowers, we talked for hours. The air was brisk, so he put his arms around me, shielding me from the cold.

Trying to show my excitement, I let him hold me as my inner voice said, "*Say no Janice, just say no, and walk away from him.*" I knew I was making a serious mistake. I didn't love him, but I also felt I wasn't deserving of anyone else.

I also wanted assurance that no one else would have the chance to condemn me; Bobby gave me his word that he wouldn't tell anyone about my abortion.

Bobby promised me that he would go to counseling if that's what it took, and that he had never loved anyone as he loved me. Once again, he asked if I would marry him.

My answer was yes.

Early the next evening, he handed me a tiny black box, and I knew it was a ring. Nervously, I opened the lid, and tucked inside a pocket of velvet was a gold band with a sparkling exquisite marquis diamond.

3

First Misconception: I Had the Ability to Make Him Change

Tonight is my wedding night, and now that I'm his wife,
surely he'll love me and honor the vows we shared.

Since childhood, I had dreamed of my wedding day, and finally that moment arrived. Nothing else seemed as important to me as being a wife and mother and living happily ever after in a cottage filled with love.

On June 17, 1978, the morning of my wedding, yet another feeling of caution and dread came over me. As I sat on the edge of my bed, my eyes fixed on my wedding gown. As if in a trance, my fingers lingered over its softness. Shouldn't my heart beat with excitement and anticipation? Shouldn't my face reflect a bride's radiant glow? I wondered.

This was to be my wedding day. A day once asleep in quiet slumber had finally awakened, no longer a dream but reality.

Knowing it was too late to change my mind, I quickly silenced my foolish heart.

My thoughts returned to my sister's wedding gown, simple in design and yet splendid in its sweet and sacred reverence.

Wild and frantic thoughts pulsated through my heart. How had I arrived at this day so ill-prepared in really knowing what was best for me?

Why did Bobby and I meet?

The feelings of fear and attraction simultaneously pulled me into his dark world. Was it fate? Why didn't I run when I had the chance?

Silencing my doubts, I tried on my veil as I held the gown up to myself. Still, my mind wandered far away. Softly I wiped away my tears, telling myself they didn't mean anything, brides are notoriously nervous on their wedding day. But nothing felt real, least of all my feelings.

The morning flew by, and soon it was time to meet with my family at the chapel. As I walked into the foyer, I once again felt a silent reminder that I didn't have to marry Bobby; the choice was still mine to make, but I was without the courage to run. Instead, with the organ playing, I walked down the aisle and confronted a man with two different faces. One face desperately desired to conquer his demons, and the other revealed an inner child of rage. Holding my brother's arm, I felt my world slip away as Bobby's hand reached out to me.

Slowly we turned to face the bishop. Bobby promised to love, honor, and cherish me as his wife, and in return, I promised to obey him as my lawfully wedded husband, and with those words I looked into his eyes and said, "I do."

Our evening was filled with excitement. Relatives painted Bobby's car with the words "Just Married" and tied the traditional tin cans to the bumper. We had a wonderful time that evening, and Bobby revealed a very affectionate and loving side to him as he proudly introduced his bride to friends and relatives. Once the guests were gone, Bobby and I gathered a few of our belongings and left for California. We were both excited and behaved like any other couple just married, in love and on their way to spend a few days on their honeymoon.

It was late in the evening and we were both exhausted but having fun talking and listening to music. We had both become quiet for a minute when his driving made me nervous enough to timidly say, "Honey, don't you think you're driving a little too fast?"

That's all it took. He hit the brakes so suddenly the car came to a screeching halt in the middle of the freeway.

The smell of burnt rubber permeated the air, and soda cans and melting ice spilled onto the floor of the backseat. Before I had a chance to react, he grabbed me by the hair and bashed my head against the dashboard.

Screaming obscenities, he yelled, "Don't you ever tell me how to drive again, do you understand?"

Scared out of my wits, I immediately pulled away from him. We were in the middle of the desert just outside of Palm Springs, so I was at his mercy. The shock that such a simple request angered him enough to instantly react, grab my hair and force my head against the dashboard made me feel sick. And on our honeymoon!

Quickly he surveyed the backseat of his car, became livid at the sight, and demanded that I clean it up. I climbed into the backseat, furious and humiliated, holding back tears as I cleaned out the car. My head was hurting, and I felt the swelling from the bruises that were already starting to form. We drove the rest of the way in silence. I didn't dare say a word.

Early the next morning, we arrived in Anaheim. We checked into a motel, and I felt the hostility between us. I couldn't believe the terrible mistake I had made when I married him. There I was in the motel lobby, on my honeymoon, wishing the bridegroom would die of a sudden heart attack. This was worse than anything I had ever imagined.

After a few days at Disneyland, we drove to San Diego. We only stayed over one night, but I loved the view of the ocean and longed for my husband's gentle touch. Alone I walked along the beach, feeling the waves wash up against the shore. Each wave seemed to crash inward, gathering my pain and releasing it as it washed back into the sea. If I thought it would be easier to walk away from him after we married, I was mistaken. The soft breeze lifted my spirit and the moisture in the air cleansed my face.

I came upon a secluded area of rocks. No one was around. For a moment, I was able to pour out my heart asking for forgiveness. I prayed that I could be the wife my husband needed.

Everything I'd longed for since childhood was tangled up in this horrible mess. He said he'd longed for someone to love him too, yet when I was affectionate he pushed me away. Early on, he said he was sorry for hurting me. He sent bouquets of roses and opened his heart to his painful past. Now he shut me out, completely ignoring me and knowingly inflicting pain.

While we were dating, Bobby appeared to be a man of success. He dressed impeccably in designer suits and shoes that cost more than my whole wardrobe. The diamond on his finger always drew attention. He bragged about his success in commercial real estate, and from the time we met, he lavished me with flowers, gifts and dinners out. However, a few days after we returned from our honeymoon, I discovered that he was penniless.

We argued over money; in fact, we argued over everything. No matter what I did, he complained and found constant fault with me.

In search of a job, I found a part-time one with an attorney close by. My hours were flexible, but it gave me a little money of my own and time away from Bobby and the apartment.

Bobby was volatile. I knew that before I married him, but I honestly believed once I became his wife, he wouldn't feel so threatened about losing me. But it took several months of constant fault-finding and bickering before his mood finally changed. Suddenly, he was pleasant to be around and started taking me out to dinner and buying small gifts for me. We would double-date with friends from our church, but it never failed: as soon as we were around other people, he would put me down.

Every time he hurt me, I wanted him to see me cry. I wanted him to feel my pain. I wanted him to feel bad for what he had done, but instead of feeling bad he ridiculed me for crying. "Poor little baby," he would sneer. "You just want me to feel sorry for you, but I don't." Instead, he was angry that I was so weak.

Almost daily, I planned how I was going to get away from him.

It was as though he knew my plans. He emptied my wallet of any spare money I had. He locked all the windows to the apartment, kept the spare key to his car, and would take away my apartment key every time we had an argument.

Bobby sold real estate, and one afternoon he couldn't find a client's earnest money deposit. He accused me of losing it. He stormed into the house trashing everything in sight. Frightened, I started looking for it with him. The check wasn't anywhere. I always panicked when he was like this, and I had good reason. He grabbed me by the arm and began twisting it. He demanded to know what I had done with the check.

"Let go of me," I begged. "I haven't seen it."

Slapping my face, he yelled, "Find that check or else!"

He let go of my arm and shoved me into the bedroom. He pulled a drawer out and dumped the contents on the floor. Shoving me to my knees, he towered over me, demanding that I search through scattered papers.

When I didn't find it, he grabbed me by the arm and threw me across the room.

"Just find it!" he yelled.

My heart pounding, I rifled through the closet, throwing things around the room. I even tried begging him to calm down. I was scared, but he was blocking the doorway, trapping me inside.

Like a chicken with its head cut off, I scurried around the bedroom. Searching inside drawers and pulling books off the shelves, I became hysterical, knowing that I wasn't going to find it.

Sobbing, I pleaded, "I've never seen the check, Bobby. I didn't put it anywhere."

That's when he struck me. The sting of his hand made my head reel and instantly brought tears to my eyes. My cheek burned, and instinctively, I wanted to fight back. Instead, I clenched my fists and closed my eyes, waiting for the next blow.

I turned around to face him, tears streaming down my face. "I don't know where it is!"

Then the phone rang. He stopped yelling long enough to answer it. It was the escrow officer, asking Bobby if he had located the client's check.

I heard Bobby say he was still looking, and he would soon leave for the office. The moment he put the phone down, he returned to stand over me.

Irate, he said I made him look like a fool.

I was sobbing as he walked toward the door. When I heard the door close behind him, I bawled. I touched my face; it felt tender and sore as I brushed away my tears. My back hurt, and it was difficult to move.

Outraged, I ran into the bathroom to wash my face.

Then I knew what I had to do. A light clicked on inside my brain. I didn't have to take it; I could get the hell out.

I grabbed a suitcase and threw in some clothes as fast as I could, scared half to death that he would catch me before I had time to escape.

Each time I threw a sweater or pair of jeans into my suitcase; I panicked and ran around in circles.

My adrenaline was pumping, and I was shaking like a leaf. I ran to the window, trying to see outside to the parking lot, and then I hurried back into the bedroom and continued emptying out my drawers. Then it dawned on me: I wasn't prepared to leave. I had no money, no car, and nowhere to go.

Suddenly, the front door flew open. His intrusion brought me back to reality, and I couldn't hide my suitcase fast enough.

Furiously he threw me onto the bed, grabbing me by the hair. He put his face in mine and said, "If you leave me, I swear I'll tell everyone you had an abortion."

My hands ached to reach up and slap his face. I was so angry with myself for not running out the front door screaming for help. Did it really matter whether I had a place to go? Sleeping on the streets would have been safer.

How could anyone hurt another person the way he would hurt me? God, I hated him! I was emotionally exhausted from hurting so deep. Inside my heart, my wounds were bleeding.

Throwing my head back against the bed, he released his hold and walked out of the room.

Once I heard the front door slam, I knew he was gone. I was no longer scared; my anguish and sorrow broke through a dam of repression. In agony, I prayed, "What's wrong with you, God? Why won't you help me?"

Unable to stop the tears, I cried until I was exhausted. I stayed in bed the rest of the afternoon. When I awoke, it was dark in my bedroom. The sun was setting, and I felt night drawing near. Gloom filtered out the soft glow of the sun just before it dipped beneath the earth, and I felt damp with desolation.

I'm not living anymore, I sobbed. I felt dead inside, as fear and darkness enveloped me.

Later that night, Bobby returned home with a beautiful bouquet of red roses, as if that would erase the horror he'd caused.

He was despicable, and yet each time he put his arms around me, I allowed him—and I pretended to love him. He apologized for his volatile behavior that afternoon and casually admitted the check he accused me of losing had been clipped to a file inside his briefcase.

Silently, I whispered, *"Just don't feel anything, Janice, least of all your pain."* Then for a moment, I allowed myself to believe he really did feel sorry. The bouquet of roses meant he loved me that he was sorry— but in reality, I hurt too much to care. I accepted the roses just like I always did to prevent another argument.

One afternoon, sick of being blamed for everything, I stood up to him when he started throwing unpaid bills in my face. Shaking but indignant that I was being blamed, I shouted, "The only reason we don't have any money is because you aren't making any."

Slowly he took a few steps toward me, like a wildcat sneaking up on his prey, but I didn't move away from him. I was going to fight back this time.

Looking me straight in the eye, he sarcastically said, "Do you want to repeat what you just said?"

At that moment I did, so I answered him, "When you bring home a paycheck, Bobby, our bills will be paid."

First he hit me with both hands against my shoulders, shoving me backward, and then he dared me to say it one more time. That's when I regretted opening my mouth. I frantically tried to take the words back. I really was sorry for saying them, not because they weren't true, but because I had provoked him.

With one blow, he knocked me to the floor and started throwing punches. Terrified, I was screaming, but this didn't stop him.

The wind knocked out of me, I lay helpless as he kicked me one last time and told me to get up. Humiliated, I slowly picked myself up off the floor. By his tone, I knew he was finished for now and I was free to walk away.

The sun was sinking below the earth as my heart was sinking below the deepest portion of my being. What a poor wretched woman I had become, trapped like a bird with broken wings. I desperately wanted love, and I was tired of living on the hope that tomorrow he would be someone different. I wanted to fly away on moonlit beams to a place that offered me a minute's peace, but instead of taking power away from him, a timid voice, one I knew to be my enemy, silenced any courage I had. In its place was left a whining little girl frantically begging for someone to answer her, *"Where will I go, how will I ever get away from him?"*

I walked into the bathroom, unable to look at myself as I meticulously got dressed for bed. Pouring my thoughts into what I was doing, feeling too tired to think or run, hurting over every inch of my body, I finally glanced into the mirror and saw the bruises. I touched my body and felt the physical pain, but nothing compared to my despair. I crawled meekly into bed, silently praying that by morning this nightmare would go away. Somehow, I would come up with a plan.

I waited until he was asleep. I carefully got out of bed and searched through his briefcase until I found a check. Would it be enough to cover a plane ticket? I didn't care. I took the check and carefully tucked it in a pair of shoes.

The next morning, he awoke and dressed for work feeling satisfied that I had nowhere else to go. But this time, he was wrong. I felt brave enough to ask a neighbor I barely knew to give me a ride to the airport. I bought a one-way ticket to Salt Lake City. I would stay with my sister until I could figure things out.

4

Religion's Myth of Saving the Family

Listen to the whispering in your heart; listen before it's too late.
There's only one choice to make—do it for yourself!

In the fall of '78, my sister Diane was attending Brigham Young University in Provo, and my mother was visiting with her family in the Utah area. Once I arrived, I told my mom everything.

I must have been undecided, even though I swore I would never return to him, because I called Bobby a few days later. I wanted him to know that I was far enough away from him and this time I wasn't coming home.

I didn't owe him the courtesy of a phone call, but perhaps I just wanted to hear him beg for mercy or say how sorry he was.

It's possible that in my delusional thinking I really didn't want a divorce; I just wanted him to change. But the memory of his violent temper, his rage, and the beatings spoke for themselves.

Bobby wasn't going to change, and I knew that. Over the next few days, we spent hours on the phone talking, but a silent voice kept on whispering, *"Leave him, Janice, and you will be okay"*.

His remorse and the sound of his weeping didn't change my

mind at first. I had made up my mind, and I wasn't coming home. That's when he threatened to kill himself. I sensed his despondency, and I really believed he would do it, so I gave him my sister's phone number.

A day or two later, I was still in Provo when I received a phone call from a counselor in the bishopric. Bobby had been to see him and was "more repentant and humble," he said, than anyone he had counseled before.

"Your husband is severely depressed and I'm quite worried about him. He is threatening suicide." He went on to say, "He deeply regrets the harm he caused you."

I spent hours explaining to him in detail about Bobby's violent behavior. I wanted him to understand the abuse I had suffered physically, mentally, and emotionally. "But Janice," he said, "Bobby loves you. He hasn't stopped crying or left his apartment for work since you walked out on him, and I feel he really is suicidal."

He also agreed with me when he said, "Your husband does have problems, but he is willing to work on them, and he has agreed to go to counseling. He is willing to do anything to save this marriage. Divorce is not always the answer; you need to consider the vows you made and be willing to honor them and look toward the future, toward a temple sealing. This will change both your lives."

I didn't want to return, but I felt sorry for Bobby's suffering and foolish enough to believe in this man, "called by God," to guide me.

After months of living with someone as volatile and unremorseful as my husband, I had somehow found the courage to leave. It was the right thing to do, and in my heart I knew it. At first, my husband had almost convinced me that I was crazy and responsible for his temper—I was the one who caused him to get angry and hurt me. I even believed at times that I could change him by changing my behavior. But even if I had problems, I wasn't safe with him, so

I didn't understand why someone else was siding with him and pressuring me to return, and why this counselor had enough power over me to convince me that I should.

Deep inside, I had no doubt that if I returned to Bobby; I would never again find the courage to leave him.

It took a several weeks of phone calls before this same counselor convinced me and others my marriage was worth saving. I needed to give Bobby a second chance before leaving him.

He told me about the first time he met Bobby, and how impressed he was that this man was willing to do anything just to turn things around and be active in the church.

But most of all, he said, Bobby wanted a temple marriage. The counselor reminded me that to be married in the temple, Bobby would have to be worthy; therefore, he would need to get his life in order.

"This is something you can both work toward," he said, reminding me that I had my own problems to work on.

He was right; my membership had not been reinstated, and neither had my blessings.

Then he said, "Shouldn't this be a time you work on your problems together? Bobby is willing, shouldn't you be also?" I knew what he was referring to; he was one of the three men who held the church court disfellowshipping me for the abortion just months before my wedding.

I agonized over the decision, and for once I needed to hear, "Janice, follow your heart, you know what you need to do." But I had been so conditioned during my life to listen and follow the counsel of my church leaders that I didn't listen to myself.

Later that week, reluctant and frightened, I boarded the plane.

When the plane landed in Arizona, Bobby was waiting. In his hands was a beautiful bouquet of red roses, with delicate sprigs of baby's breath.

"I love you," he said, and as he held me in his arms he promised never to hurt me again.

Bobby was elated to have me home, or so I thought. He had a gift for me, wrapped in an expensive box from a department store, one I knew we could never afford. A stunning silk nightgown lay carefully wrapped inside. He made love to me, caressing my body and telling me how beautiful I was. He was so sorry for his behavior—he wanted to start our marriage over again.

But disconnection notices and unpaid bills were also sitting on the kitchen table, and I had to wonder if the rent had even been paid.

In the weeks that followed, we had an interview with our bishop, and he informed us that in a year, providing we did as we were told; we could be sealed in God's temple.

We were advised to faithfully attend our church meetings, hold family home evenings, pay our tithing, and be active in church callings. The bishop agreed to pay for our counseling from the ward budget, but we would have to meet with a church-approved psychiatrist.

Bobby was anxious to go; he thought counseling would help me. During our first session, Bobby used the hour to complain about what bothered him about me. The following session, the psychiatrist gently told Bobby he had a few problems to work on himself. Bobby jumped from his chair and started shaking his fist at the psychiatrist. He accused him of taking my side, and at that moment, marital counseling took a turn for the worse. In fact, it stopped.

Life with Bobby really hadn't changed either. Nothing I did according to the advice given to me by the psychiatrist made the least bit of difference. My membership with the church did change, however; after an interview with the same three men, it was determined that I had been penalized sufficiently to have my membership fully reinstated. By that time, I was pregnant. I wanted to feel joy, but the feelings weren't there. The afternoon I received the test results from my doctor's office, I was torn between excitement and anxiety.

Bobby was five years older than me and had said for years that he desperately wanted a child. I felt that having a baby would save our marriage. I must have believed that somehow the baby would do what I had not been able to—soften Bobby's anger.

Later that evening, I shared my news with Bobby. I put my arms around him and gently kissed him as I said, "Honey, I'm pregnant."

He pulled away from me and said, "Am I supposed to trust that you won't kill this baby like you did the last one?"

His coldness spoiled another moment in my life that I had always dreamed of. He had robbed me of precious moments that should have been filled with joy. I turned away to hide my tears. I didn't want him to see how deeply he had hurt me again.

Even though I was desperately unhappy, I was good at pretending otherwise. I was excited about being an expectant mother. What would it be like to give life to this baby, carry it inside me and feel it move? The world around me silenced for just a second. I sat quietly outside by the pool, feeling the heat of the Arizona sun. The air, filled with sweet fragrant orange blossoms, reminded me of the days when I first arrived in Arizona. My hopes and dreams had slowly shattered, and the choices that followed changed my life forever. Reality, as cruel as it can sometimes be, reminded me how precarious elusive dreams really are—but on that day, I promised God that I would not fail Him as a mother.

No matter how much my husband reminded me of my failings, I knew I would be a loving mother. For weeks, all I could talk about was "the baby" and how excited I was about becoming a mother.

The marital tide turned, and for a while Bobby seemed bewildered, as if he didn't know how to behave. He stopped finding fault in me; in fact, he was calm when he spoke. He left every day for the office instead of staying home. We had friends over for dinner, and we went out to movies. The change felt like a breath of spring air flowing through open windows in a stale, smelly basement. I felt hopeful. I even believed Bobby was settling down. During this time in my marriage, I was happy. Any loving touch from my husband warmed my heart, and I gave thanks each night for soft-spoken words of kindness. How I hungered for love.

I was working part-time, and I splurged once in a while buying baby clothes and preparing a nursery. With less tension at home, I was excited to show Bobby everything new I purchased for the baby. I felt free to come and go. I honestly believed my husband would never hurt his unborn child. I even believed he felt a greater respect for me.

One hot June afternoon, when I was seven-and-a-half months pregnant, Bobby wanted me to go for a ride with him. We had just entered the freeway when he said, "I know you're planning on leaving me."

"Whatever makes you think that?" I exclaimed.

Bobby and I were getting along. He was nice. I certainly wasn't planning a way to escape, so I denied it.

Before I could absorb what was happening, he struck me across the face. I immediately panicked. I had been in the same situation before and hated being trapped in the car—it was worse than a closed-off room when he was explosive. I begged him to stop the car. All he did was scream at me louder, weaving in and out of traffic. I tried to grab the keys from the ignition, but he grabbed my hand before I could. I tried to break free, and he slammed on the brakes, pulling off to the side of the road. He slugged me hard enough in the side of my stomach to knock the wind out of me as he pulled back onto the freeway. Terrified that he had hurt the baby, I froze in my seat. I didn't dare move, but I couldn't stop screaming while Bobby was yelling.

Within minutes, he exited the freeway and found a deserted street with an empty field and apartment complex close by. He pulled over, yelling the same obscenities, telling me he would rather see us both dead than go through a divorce while I was pregnant.

At first, I refused to get out of the car. Then, thinking of the alternative, I leapt out. He immediately threw the car into reverse. Spinning his tires, he drove right for me. I screamed at him to stop, terrified he would run over me.

An empty field stood a short distance away from the apartment complex. I ran toward the apartment building screaming for help. Bobby slammed on his brakes and jumped from the car, chasing me.

I was far enough ahead that Bobby stopped and turned back. I hid inside the building's courtyard until I thought he had left.

Then I started walking home, but home was miles away.

Finally I sat down on the curb. I didn't know what else to do, but I was scared. My stomach was cramping as though labor had started, and I was extremely exhausted. I was so concerned for my baby's welfare that the tears started flowing. Sudden relief flooded me when finally I felt the baby kick.

Sobbing, I talked to the baby, telling him how sorry I was for the terrible mess our lives were in.

It was scorching hot that day, and I knew I wouldn't make it very far walking, so I waited. Sweat was dripping down my face, and I was furious with Bobby. A few hours had passed when I finally spotted his car. I waited until he drove up beside me. We were both still angry and we continued to argue, but I got back inside the car. On the way home, he gave me an ultimatum.

"I would rather see you dead than allow you to ever leave with my baby."

"You're crazy, Bobby. Is this your sick way of warning me?" I screamed back.

"Take it any way you want, but you will never leave with my

child. Once the baby is born, you can get the hell out of my life for all I care, but you will never leave with my baby."

Heartsick that I was back in the same old situation with Bobby, I had to admit to myself that nothing had changed. I despised Bobby even more knowing he was capable of endangering not only me, but also our unborn child. During the night, I started feeling bad. The cramps I felt earlier intensified, but I thought all I needed was more rest. The next morning was Sunday, and I told Bobby I didn't feel like attending church.

"You're not staying home," he said, demanding that I get dressed and show up to church with him. I did as I was told.

By noon, I was feeling contractions. We left church early, and Bobby drove me to the hospital, where I was admitted. My doctor was notified, and for several hours the nurses monitored my contractions until they determined I was in labor.

I listened as the nurses spoke among themselves. "She's too small. I don't think she is full-term." But when my doctor arrived, he didn't seem concerned. After twelve hours, the doctor broke my water—"to get this over with," he said, and it worked.

My baby was seven-and-a-half weeks early. Robby wasn't breathing and had turned blue. They worked on him for a moment, and then the nurses rushed him out of the delivery room. I was frightened, but no one would tell me what was happening. Later, a nurse told me my baby wasn't breathing on his own.

As soon as I was in my room, the doctor came in and said my baby's condition was critical. He was on oxygen, and they would need to air-evacuate him to St. Joseph's Hospital in Phoenix, which was better equipped to handle premature births.

Robby suffered from hyaline membrane disease, also known as respiratory distress syndrome. RDS occurs in babies with incomplete lung development, and it is the most common disease of premature infants.

As soon as I was released from Mesa Lutheran Hospital, Bobby and I rushed over to St. Joseph's. Even though Robby was tiny, he wasn't the smallest infant in the neonatal intensive care unit. Robby almost appeared full-term in size next to one tiny infant, Willie, who wasn't more than two pounds; quite often, a nurse would thump Willie's little chest with her finger to keep his heart beating.

I felt so terribly guilty when I watched my infant son struggle for each breath he took. He had tubes and wires connected from him to monitors, and within days his condition took a turn for the worse. His doctor reassured me that this was to be expected.

I quit my job to be with my baby as often as I could. Within two weeks, I was able to hold Robby for the first time outside the safety of his incubator. The nurse would lift him out; careful not to disturb the wires and other connections he had, and let me hold him. I spent many long hours inside the NICU, rocking my baby and listening to the monitors.

Gradually, Robby improved. His stay approximately four weeks, but Robby was still so tiny when we brought him home that I hardly slept at night, afraid he would stop breathing. I kept his bassinet right next to my bed, and often I would fall asleep with my hand inside his bed so I could touch his little chest to make sure he was still breathing.

Bobby was supportive during this time. He stopped complaining and finding fault with me. Perhaps he felt a twinge of guilt, if that's possible, that our baby was born premature. Even though I held my feelings close to me, since it never served me well to confide in Bobby, I couldn't help but feel resentful and angry with him that he had caused unnecessary harm the day before Robby's birth. Was he to blame? Was I?

A year had passed since Bobby and I said our wedding vows, and Bobby finally got the moment he had been waiting for: his temple sealing. More than anything else, he wanted to be married in the temple with the ceremony he believed would seal us together for all eternity. Since I had not only myself to think about but the baby as well, I believed it was the right thing for us to do.

We were also fortunate enough to purchase a two-story home on a cul-de-sac next to a lake. Finally we were out of the apartment I disliked, and it was a beautiful home—bright and airy with three bedrooms upstairs. It was exciting to decorate a nursery for Robby with hopes of really starting a family together.

We both made appointments to see our bishop. Bobby's appointment was separate from mine, but in my interview it was mentioned that a wife could soften the heart of her husband by her willingness to enter God's temple. By receiving the anointing of celestial blessings, our marriage would be sanctified by God. This was something missing in our civil ceremony, because it was done without the proper authority.

I listened carefully, and the words echoed the teachings of my youth. For a moment, the past no longer existed, and the abuse would be erased. The responsibility was placed on my shoulders to be kind, patient, and forgiving, to endure the trials God placed before me.

In retrospect, even to this day it amazes me that I believed in this as if I were Alice in Wonderland and had somehow fallen down the rabbit hole. I thought, just like Alice did, that I had slipped into Wonderland. In reality, Alice was a fictional character created as a "crazy" girl wandering around changing into different characters in the Underland.

And in reality, I was slipping into a dark place of my own Underland. The story you read is not fictional, and the characters are real.

5

Temple Sealing

*Is there magic inside a sacred room that softens hearts
and changes anger into love and a house into a safe haven?*

I'll never forget the morning my husband and I knelt at the
altar, and our baby was placed between us. We joined hands,
kneeling across from each other, and the officiator pronounced a
ceremony that sealed us as husband and wife "for all eternity." We
were promised many blessings if we stayed faithful to our covenants
and returned often to the temple.

First we went in for own endowments, and once we completed
each phase, we were led to the sealing room. The room was lavishly
decorated in gold and extremely elegant. Its exquisiteness was equal
to a king's palace. Crystal chandeliers and elaborate beauty in every
ornate detail took my breath away. I felt lost in a room shrouded with
secrecy. It was so easy to go along with the idealism of perfection
and righteousness in order to believe in prophetic words of eternal
promises.

I remember standing in front of a mirror that echoed my image
forever. This mirror symbolized eternity; the room symbolized

purity. I'm not sure what character I had assumed that morning, but I thought, *"How could we leave this place and not be changed?"*

Later that morning, we left with our families. Bobby was holding my hand as I held our son and walked down the front stairs of the temple. I wanted to believe his heart had also been softened after our experience that morning.

It didn't take long for that myth to be exposed for what was: deceiving and misleading.

Each day I awoke with the same burdens, yet I made my way through the day as a Mormon wife should. I did all the right things, and my home portrayed the ideals I had been taught. We both had church callings. I was just like everyone else—married in the temple and starting a family. Then I was called to serve in the Young Women's presidency, and I loved working with the young girls.

But that didn't stop the fighting. It was always over little things I did. Bobby said I spent too much time away from home. He didn't like it that I had to go to church meetings during the week. He didn't like it that I spent time with the young girls from my class. He took everything that gave me joy and spoiled it until there was nothing to savor, nothing to squeeze from the pleasure of having a life of my own.

It became increasingly difficult to carry out my responsibilities as a counselor in the presidency. I worried constantly every minute that I was away from home. Then three months after the birth of my son, I was pregnant again, complicating my situation even more. I was not ready for another pregnancy, and I struggled with the guilt I felt. In retrospect, I know I was also suffering from postpartum depression.

Bobby complained about the way I kept house so much that I became obsessed with it. The carpet pile couldn't have lines in it, and if I saw footprints during any time of the day, I would haul out that vacuum cleaner and vacuum those prints away. I scrubbed the bathrooms until it appeared as though no one used them. I would keep an eye on both of them throughout the day.

One morning, I went into the kitchen and started cleaning. Everything appeared filthy to me, and yet it was not. I tore everything from the pantry shelves, littering my kitchen floor with a huge mess, and then I scrubbed the shelves with tears streaming down my face. Soon my tears turned into wracking sobs. I sat in the middle of my floor sobbing my heart out, with swollen ankles and a stomach that made my husband laugh at me when I undressed in front of him.

Somehow, I made it through my second pregnancy—I don't know how—but nine months passed rather quickly.

Even though my baby was four weeks early, Darinn was healthy. But once he was home from the hospital, this baby cried nonstop. He was constantly fussy, and his endless crying frayed my nerves. A routine checkup with his pediatrician revealed an ear infection.

I felt guilty for the feelings I had while I was pregnant. The baby wasn't to blame, and I wanted to make that up to him.

I held him and sang soft lullabies.

I let dirty laundry pile up. My kitchen didn't have that "Mr. Clean" look to it, and that bothered Bobby.

It took time, but he didn't treat Darinn the same as he did Robby.

He was cruel to this tiny baby. If I ever had to discipline Robby, Bobby would immediately take it out on him. From the time our second baby was born, Bobby told him over and over again that his mommy didn't want him before he was born.

When the baby was only a few months old, Bobby insisted I walk away from him and let him cry because I was spoiling him by holding him. I ignored Bobby's warning until he grabbed Darinn from my arms and ran into the bedroom, locking the door behind him. He stayed inside that room as I listened to my baby scream for what seemed to be hours.

I pleaded with him to let me in. "He's just a baby," I said as I knelt sobbing by the door.

The door flew open, and Bobby grabbed me by the hair. Dragging me toward the stairs, he screamed, "I've warned you for the last time to shut up."

I tried to hold on to the railing, but with his strength he yanked me away and threw me down a flight of stairs.

"I'll never let you ruin my kids," he screamed as he watched me hitting each step. "You're not fit to be anyone's mother."

I jumped to my feet screaming like a banshee. "I *am* crazy," I yelled at the top of my lungs. "To live with you, Bobby, I would have to be crazy."

Before the reality of the repercussions for saying that hit me, I heard Bobby's thundering feet as he raced down the stairs. I may have been crazy for marrying him, but I wasn't *that* crazy. At least I knew to run for my life.

Racing for the front door, my heart nearly leapt from my chest as I grabbed the door handle. It opened, and I was out of there, leaving the door wide open.

Bobby didn't follow me. Instead, the door slammed behind me. I heard the locks click tightly into place, and I knew I would be left outside for as long as it took him to open the door and allow me to come inside my own home.

It was hot outside. I hurt, mostly from carpet burns, and my right shoulder was very tender. Unimaginable acts of cruelty usually left me in pain and crying, but this time I was angry. That was my baby he was using as a weapon against me, and Darinn was only two months old. I was afraid for my child. I felt waiting was best for me. Bobby would soon open the door, and somehow I would make a plan to run when I had both babies with me.

Even though Bobby could be kind at times, now he didn't seem to have any feeling for me at all. Constantly disrespectful, he hardly spoke a kind word, and he easily lost his patience with our two boys. I planned constantly how I would escape. Thoughts of where would I go, how, when? But he always had Rob with him. Financially I was without resources, and now I had two children to take care of. This was my home, with a nursery for the baby and a bedroom filled with toys where Rob slept. Bobby was the one who needed to change, because I needed the security and the familiarity of everything surrounding me.

Darinn was nearly nine months old when Bobby picked him up because he was crying. First he tried soothing him. He gave him a bottle and walked with him, but Darinn wouldn't stop crying.

Timidly, I asked Bobby to let me have him. I knew that it wouldn't take long before Bobby lost his temper. But he only shoved me aside and then started violently shaking the baby.

In a fit of rage, Bobby threw Darinn hard enough that the baby bounced off the bed and hit the floor. Racing toward him, I picked him up as Bobby stood there staring at him. At first, nothing seemed to be really wrong with him. I laid him down on the bed and then we both saw—his little arm was broken.

"Look what you've done to this baby," I screamed.

Instantly, Bobby slapped me across the face; he swore he'd beat the life out of me if I ever accused him of hurting the baby.

"It was an accident. That's all it was." We rushed Darinn to the emergency room and the doctor put on a cast.

I never told a soul that Bobby broke the baby's arm.

I am so sorry for this. Even though it sounds so meaningless today, I didn't say a word about what happened that afternoon. Even while in the ER, when questions were asked about how the baby's arm was broken, I didn't dare say anything except what we both agreed would be our story.

I had to go home with Bobby that night; I didn't know where else I would go. I was afraid of the unknown and afraid of what I absolutely knew would happen. My voice was silenced as Bobby did all the talking.

With every incident that happened there was always hope it wouldn't happen again. Hope that he would actually feel bad enough and change or just the plain inability to admit it was never going to stop. Either way, it's a frightening reality, a common dysfunctional behavior that must be treated as an illness. Without intervention and acts of prevention that include healing mind, body, and spirit, change won't mean anything. Hope begins within the human spirit, the mind, and the sacred heart, and it's being destroyed in countless lives today.

6

The Abuse Only Gets Worse

Battering isn't an isolated incident.
If it happens once, it will happen again

It was a blistering summer afternoon, hot as it always is during August in Mesa, when Bobby and I took the boys for a ride.

Abruptly, something I said irritated him. He started yelling at me in the middle of traffic.

Our windows were rolled down because of the lack of air-conditioning in our car, and I was embarrassed when others turned to stare at us.

When we stopped at a red light, I tried to quiet him down while he raged at my stupidity. The light soon changed to green, and recklessly he kept driving as we both continued to argue.

I always felt I needed to defend myself—prove to him that I wasn't an imbecile.

"I'm not stupid, Bobby," I said. "Why do you always say that?"

We continued fighting until the boys began crying. That's when he stopped the car and forced me to get out.

I watched the car disappear out of sight. Standing in traffic, I was boiling mad and bawling like a baby. Then I started walking. I walked, but not toward home. I walked in circles, not knowing where I would go. Scared for my babies and hurting beyond measure, I wanted to pound my fists into my chest. Something inside was going to explode. Bobby was starting to get into a really bad habit of using my children to hurt me, and it didn't bother him. I knew I would have to go home sooner or later—he had my children. I didn't have my purse with me, and I wasn't about to stop at anyone's home and call him. And I certainly wasn't going to call anyone else I knew.

It took me an hour or so walking in the heat of the afternoon sun until I finally reached the edge of my driveway. The car was parked in the garage, but the front door was locked. I stood outside knocking on the door, begging Bobby to let me in.

He finally answered, opening the door only a crack. "What the hell do you want?"

Quietly, I answered him, "I want in, Bobby."

He stared at me for a moment and then left the door open. Muttering under his breath, he said, "Whatever."

A few days later, we received a foreclosure notice in the mail. Bobby hit the ceiling. "What in the hell are we going to do?" he screamed at me.

Waving the certified letter in my face, he blamed me for the mess we were in.

Then he let me have it. Bobby hit me across the face, knocking me to the ground. As I felt the sting, tears sprang to my eyes. Hating him, I didn't dare stand up or react in any way. Curled in a fetal position, I couldn't help but silence my rage with self-blame.

A few weeks later, I remember strapping Robby and Darinn into their car seats and leaving for Circle K to pick up a few things we needed.

I was exhausted that morning. I had been up most of the night with both babies. Both kids were fussy, and my nerves were on edge.

If I had only stopped to listen to the alarm bells ringing in my head, maybe I would have realized that I was on stress overload.

The minute I drove into our garage, I took Darinn out of his car seat and released Robby from his. Unable to carry babies, milk, and a few bags of food into the house, I opted to leave Robby still sitting in his car seat in the back of the car for just a few seconds.

As soon as I put the milk in the refrigerator, Darinn started crying and Bobby yelled at me. We got into an argument, and I completely forgot about Robby.

Minutes later, I panicked when I looked around and didn't see Robby in the room with us. I ran into the garage, but it was empty. No car, no Robby, just an empty garage. I ran frantically down the street, but there was no sign of my car or my baby.

My first thought was that someone had stolen my car, but the second I turned around to run back home, I saw a tiny fraction of the back end of my car's trunk just before it sank to the bottom of the lake on the other side of our street.

Robby had taken the gear out of "park," and the car rolled down the embankment and into the lake.

I screamed for help, and a nearby neighbor and Bobby heard me. Bobby and the neighbor jumped into the lake and started swimming toward the car. I ran into the house and dialed 911. Soon police cars and fire trucks lined my street. The car was at the bottom of the lake before anyone was able to break the back window and bring Robby up to the surface.

Miraculously, Robby was unhurt in the accident.

Once my baby was safely in my arms, a news reporter from a local television station wanted to interview me. He caught Bobby on camera, but I quickly ran into the house. I wasn't sure what the law did to mothers who left their babies inside a parked car, but I was too ashamed to talk to anyone.

Later that night, I wept as I held Robby tight. I couldn't believe I left my baby alone even for a few seconds.

Our insurance company refused to pay for our water-damaged car, so we found an attorney that would file a lawsuit against them on our behalf. We had our car repaired as best we could afford, but the interior smelled mildewed and dank, and the car never ran again without belching exhaust like a chimney. In fact; most of the time it didn't run at all. Consequently, Bobby spent less time selling real estate than he did before.

I hated my life, and the tension was building between Bobby and me. He was always underfoot. I wanted him as far away from me as possible, but he smothered me with his foul moods and deplorable temper. Several months later, I borrowed money from my brother and my mother to put down on another mortgage, which Bobby assumed.

We were given six months before the foreclosure sale on the house we were in, but since we found another home, we decided to move right away. Bobby found someone else to assume our mortgage, and the buyer was supposed to make up the back payments.

Not too soon after we moved, I discovered that I was pregnant with my third baby. Bobby had been in an automobile accident, rupturing a disk. For several months, he was in physical therapy and not working. Making an appointment with our bishop, I went in to see him alone.

I broke down. Pouring my heart out, I told him of the abuse and Bobby's inability to support his family. The counsel I was given was to keep doing my best.

"We don't believe in divorce," he said, "but I do agree that you and Bobby need counseling." I tried to explain that counseling hadn't worked in the past, but I was encouraged to attend the temple and pay my tithes and offerings, and we would be blessed.

However, the bishop was willing to give us assistance. Completely dependent on church welfare, I thought I had reached the lowest point in my entire life.

It was so humiliating to take my food order and drive to the church storehouse. I would have to hand over the approved form to a person who was in charge that day. This individual would walk with me, making sure I only picked those items on my list. That didn't make me feel any better, and if I saw someone there from my ward volunteering, I would drive home without picking up my desperately needed food.

I was in my seventh month when labor started. My doctor put me on bed rest. For weeks I stayed in bed. Friends in my neighborhood helped take care of my boys, and a good friend would help me with my laundry and housecleaning. But it was always about Bobby and his needs.

Later during the week, he was complaining about my inability to work to help take the stress off him or take care of the house, and even though I knew I shouldn't, I screamed back at him, letting him know he had failed me. Even this home would soon go into foreclosure if he wasn't able to sell real estate. We were already on church welfare. I was pregnant, and I was sick of him. I'd had enough, but at that moment, I broke a battered woman's most cardinal rule: never make your husband angry when he has access to any kind of weapon.

He grabbed a golf club, and before I could run, he hit me just below my knees. With shattering pain I fell to the floor, but the second blow came before I could move. As I crawled across the floor, he hit me again and again.

The boys were playing with their toys, and I screamed at them to run into their room and lock the door. They didn't hesitate. They ran as fast as their little legs could carry them and quickly slammed the bedroom door. Bobby never stopped hitting me. Suddenly, my pain didn't matter. My only thoughts were, *"What if he hits the baby?"*

I doubled over screaming as I tried to protect my unborn baby. Immediately, I felt a blow across my back.

Bobby screamed, "Get up," but I didn't move. He wouldn't stop beating me.

One leg and hip was feeling the brunt of each forceful swing, and I screamed over and over, begging him to stop. My back, hip, and leg were severely throbbing with pain, but Bobby laughed and said, "If you could only see how pathetic you look. You're a stupid weak bitch that doesn't know when to stop."

Once he stopped swinging that awful club at me, he threw it across the room and walked away. I could hear my boys crying behind their door and screaming for their daddy to stop, but I couldn't go to them. On hands and knees, I crawled into the bathroom, unable to stand.

This was a turning point for me.

I wasn't angry with Bobby like I had been in the past, because I expected his abuse. I had lived that way for so many years; it had become part of a sick marital ritual. This time, in all my wounded pain, I was angry with myself.

I grabbed a pair of scissors from the bathroom drawer. Not knowing exactly what I was going to do with them, I screamed at Bobby, begging him to answer me.

"What have you done to me?" Carefully, I slipped off my pants, but I was in terrible pain.

Half of my body was so badly beaten it looked like a slab of meat, black and blue and purple and quickly swelling. Immediately I took off my maternity top and carefully examined my stomach. Bobby's blows had not touched the baby. I was so angry and sobbing violently.

I wanted to hurt myself. I thought about slashing my wrists, but with a dull pair of scissors, I knew that wouldn't work. In sheer desperation, I even wanted to stab myself, but it was my face that kept looking back at me every time I peeked into the mirror.

Only God knew how deeply I hated that pathetic face. I wanted her to go away, but she wouldn't stop staring at me. Silence filled the air; I couldn't hear a sound. I wasn't crying anymore. Instead, I was gazing deep into my bathroom mirror, and the image looking back at me was of a woman I hated.

I wanted her to die. This hopelessly brainless woman had haunted me for years.

Helplessly, she cried out, and in anger she stormed about ranting and raving, but not once did she walk out the front door and never return.

Even though I hated the sight of this pitiful woman, I knew she had won. The woman living in the attic of my mind was my enemy, and somehow she had invaded my body and was living my life. It was me who was dying every time she took the abuse, and I realized how much I deeply, deeply hated myself.

I took the scissors and cut off chunks of my hair. Then I really looked hideous, and I couldn't help but let the tears begin again. In a fit of fury, I smashed the mirror, and as it shattered into tiny pieces, I turned to God and once again begged him to answer me: "Why, God, why is this happening to me?"

I made my way into the kitchen, fixed a bag of ice, and hobbled into my bedroom. As I tried to lie down on the bed, I hurt so badly I had to stay in one position, so I placed the ice where it hurt the most. I could hear Bobby in the bathroom walking on broken glass.

"Don't even come near me," I screamed at Bobby. "I swear I'll kill you if you touch me one more time." He didn't seem to care as he wandered back into the kitchen and fixed himself a sandwich.

I could hear him open the door to the boys' bedroom. Bobby told them to come out, and I knew he was bringing them into our bedroom. They were terrified as they came closer to me. They were almost too afraid to look at me when Bobby offered to take them out for a treat. "How about going with me for some ice cream?" he said, as though it was party time.

Without saying a word, my two little boys took their daddy's hand as he reached out for them. They both stopped and turned around to look at me. The look in their eyes still haunts me today.

"Don't look at your mom, she's a little crazy," he said. "Let's leave her alone to see if she can calm down. She's not really hurt; she just wants us to feel sorry for her."

All three of them walked out my bedroom door and piled into the car as Bobby drove them to Dairy Queen. "I hate you, Bobby," I mouthed the words. "Someday you will pay for what you've done to me."

7

What Makes a Battered Woman Stay?

In a world of dreams and fairy tales,
Little girls have fun with make-believe, but sometimes grown-up girls
Close their eyes to truth and pretend for as long as they can.

I wasn't living in a world of make believe. I no longer hoped that Bobby would change. I was simply trying to survive from one day to the next.

Although the swelling and bruising were still there from the terrible beating Bobby had given me, they weren't as bad as in the beginning.

Justin was born on May 25, 1982. After I was admitted into the hospital, a nurse saw my leg and wanted an explanation. I made up some silly excuse, and as she left the room, she said, "If you ever want to tell me the truth, I will listen."

I didn't trust her any more than I trusted anyone else. What advice, given to me in the past, had ever served me well? I shared my secrets with those I trusted, and as humiliating as that was, I was still with my husband. Now I was having another baby. Where would I go? Who would take in a mother with three children? So many irrational thoughts ran through my mind constantly. I believed they were true, and it is shaming for others to know. But it was the self-worthlessness and giving in each time after I left, as well as the conditioning to, "keep up the pretense," and be like everyone else that also played a part in it.

As a family, we seemed normal on Sunday as we worshipped together. We dressed and looked the part, which contributed to the denial of what was happening. Even exposing Bobby's behavior to my leaders put the responsibility back on me, so even that became part of a dysfunctional outer circle of our family as well. But also, once a woman leaves and then returns—and I'm not just referring to me but to all of us who share the same experience—we lose trust in ourselves. We begin to live through the feelings of the abuser, and it's as though one little voice timidly says, *"Leave him just one more time,"* and the other voice boldly says, *"Why? You'll just return!"*

It takes tremendous courage to leave in the first place, and if you do then return, the abuse worsens.

Also, women of my faith (at least during my generation) were taught to have many children. Birth control was never taught—abstaining from sex, yes, until after marriage, but birth control would prevent having children, and as women we were to procreate! I'm not making light of that. Motherhood is an honor. It is a privilege to give birth, but it is also a responsibility and a choice as to when and how many.

I left the hospital with no one knowing my husband was violently abusing me. Instead, we both took home our third son. I stayed home for a while. Bobby had back surgery, so that had him down for a while. It also kept him from working, but our mortgage was paid through church welfare for a little while longer.

One afternoon, a friend who lived in our ward told me about a job opening as an assistant marketing director for a home builder. I was hired and went to work full time while Bobby stayed home with the kids. After a few months, I realized I could attend night school for my real-estate license while I still had a salary coming in. This was the opportunity I really needed. Within a few months, I passed my real-estate exam.

This was a huge accomplishment for me. I then went on to list a new home subdivision, which was something to really be proud of. I was inexperienced, yet I signed a contract seasoned realtors worked years to achieve. Soon I was not only listing homes for sale but now I was the listing agent of a new home subdivision of 120 lots.

Just as I was finding a little bit of success, my husband found more reasons to find fault and criticize me. I was angry because he was out of work; he was resentful because I went to work.

He hated that I was doing well. Soon he began criticizing my work. He said I didn't know how to fill out contracts or how to work with buyers. As soon as he was feeling better, he decided he was much smarter than I was. He said he was afraid I would lose my clients, so he went with me when I met with them. Soon he talked me into turning my buyers over to him, letting him be the selling agent.

Still, together we were not making enough money to take over the payments of our mortgage, and we had to let the house go into foreclosure. Bobby always found a way to find someone to make a deal with, and this time it was his brother. He qualified for a loan for us, and we moved once again.

My neighbor volunteered to watch Robby and Darinn. Even though I didn't really know Sara and her husband, they seemed to be a trustworthy and religious family. Since Robby had started kindergarten, he was only at Sara's for half a day.

Robby and Darinn, who had just turned five and four respectively, did not adjust to the changes in their lives. Within several months, they were both angry and didn't want to be left at Sara's. It was a struggle to get them to stay, but I had to work, even though I felt guilty leaving them.

Early in the morning when I dropped them off, they would beg me not to make them stay with "that lady." At night, they cried and often had bad dreams. Darinn started wetting the bed, and Robby destroyed almost every toy he had. So much violence had gone on inside our home that I didn't pay attention to sudden changes in their behavior.

After work one day, I stopped by Sara's to pick up the boys. We were standing outside talking when Robby ran out into the street, chasing a basketball.

Andy, Sara's husband, yelled at him to get out of the street. Robby ran to me crying hysterically. He grabbed me around my knees and held on to me tightly. I was baffled at his reaction, and I told Andy that he had really frightened Robby. When Robby wouldn't stop crying, I excused us and went home.

That incident bothered me, but since I didn't understand Robby's behavior I let it go. Nearly a year had gone by since Bobby and I moved into our home on Inverness, and for almost that long I had been leaving Robby and Darinn with Sara. Within a few short days, my life was to be changed forever again.

One afternoon, Donna, a friend who lived around the corner from me, paid me a visit. She thought I should know that her five-year-old son had innocently walked in on her while she was taking a shower. Before she could say anything, he said, "Mommy, I love you so much I could just kiss your pee-pee."

Shocked, Donna hurried and dressed and then sat down with Alex. She wanted him to explain why he had said what he did. She had never heard him say things like this before, and it was a peculiar thing for a child to say.

Without hesitation, Alex answered her, "Because Matt does it to me all the time." Matt was the sixteen-year-old son of Andy and Sara. Alex continued to tell his mother how Matt and his friend would take several of the neighborhood boys to a park inside the subdivision. There was a large drainage pipe where they would all go inside, and the older boys would have the younger boys fondle them and perform oral sex.

Robby and Darinn often rode their bikes in the neighborhood, and Alex went with them. Usually, they were all together in a group. Heidi, my friend who watched Justin, allowed her two boys, the same age as mine, to play with the same group. That night, I took both my boys for a ride. We went for ice cream, and then on the way home I asked them about Matt and if he had inappropriately touched either one of them.

We talked about "good" and "bad" touches. Robby fidgeted with his ice cream, smearing it all over the car. I continued talking to them when suddenly Robby crawled into a fetal position on the floor of the car and started crying.

Darinn said, "I can't tell you, Mommy. You'll be in trouble if I do." I couldn't get them to say anything, but deep in my heart I knew, without a doubt, that they had been sexually abused and had both been traumatized.

All three mothers—Donna, Heidi, and I—got together and decided to make a police report. Alex was the only one willing to talk, and he told his mom that Matt and his friend did it to all of the kids, including mine.

I called the police and Mona, a detective for the Mesa Police Department, was assigned to the case. She interviewed all the alleged victims, and I went with my boys when it was their turn. Mona took each one of them separately into a dark and very small room without any windows; it almost resembled a prison cell.

It was an interrogation room used primarily for adults. Mona was large in stature and abrasive in her mannerisms, and these interviews with my children went on for several weeks. Sometimes they would admit that yes, something had happened; other times, they would say absolutely nothing. Each time they came out of the interrogation room, I could see how traumatized they were. I was furious with Mona.

"You can't interview these little children like they are adult criminals."

She wouldn't listen. Instead, she said, "Well, I don't think anything has even happened to your boys, because they won't talk. As for Alex, it was nothing more than innocent play between two curious boys."

Knowing she was wrong, I sought out a reputable counselor who specialized in sexual abuse. Adele was wonderful with the boys. She took her time and brought them into her center where she had toys, colorful wallpaper, games, and small child-size chairs and tables. She also had anatomically correct dolls to help the boys explain what happened to them. The other mothers brought their children to Adele, and she concluded that, in her professional opinion, the alleged perpetrators had sexually abused these boys.

Mona reopened the case when, completely unexpectedly, Robby told her that Andy, Matt's father also put things in his bottom.

When Robby was asked to describe what "things," he innocently said, "I don't know, but it felt like a telephone."

That did it with Mona. She laughed when she said, "Janice, a man doesn't put a telephone inside bottoms."

"You're right, Mona," I answered sarcastically, "but a child this age doesn't know how to describe a penis."

Any fool would know that Robby didn't actually mean a "telephone." Mona was offended by what I said, and from that moment on we really didn't get along. Later, the county attorney referred to her report as being "inept." Because of her sloppy investigation, too many mistakes had been made and it would be difficult at best to prosecute anyone.

Adele continued working with my boys. We were heartsick when the final outcome revealed this entire family had systematically abused Robby and Darinn for nearly a year.

Armed with new evidence, Bobby and I demanded the police fully investigate the allegations. Mona requested that my children have a medical exam. We took them to a doctor who had worked in the emergency room back east and had experience with sexual abuse cases. A rectal exam revealed extensive scar tissue, resulting from an object large enough to penetrate their rectum repeatedly.

Andy had been a minister at one time, and his family was highly regarded in the neighborhood. As a family, they went door to door explaining what Bobby and I had accused them of. The neighborhood took sides, and the majority of them could not believe this nice family could do such a thing. It wasn't just a police matter; it became a neighborhood nightmare. My children were ridiculed, teased by other adults and children in the neighborhood, and Andy was brave enough to openly threaten my boys if they said another word.

The investigation was a complete travesty, and the police department knew it. Mona waited too long and let things get out of hand. Infuriated, Adele agreed to go with me to pay a visit to Mesa's mayor. Somehow a local television station got wind of it and showed up on the front steps of the City Building. The mayor promised his full cooperation. What else could he say with a camera in his face?

The alleged perpetrators were never prosecuted. Charges were never filed. Mona turned the situation around one afternoon when she took me aside and told me I was the real fool. "Your children are accusing the wrong man," she said.

As a result of the medical exam, and since my two children were the only ones who underwent the exam, it was her opinion that the sexual abuse happened inside our home. It was her opinion that it just wasn't possible for someone else to have this kind of access to children, even though she knew they were in Sara's care at least six hours every day for one year.

Did Mona scare me? You bet she did. I didn't know who to believe. I never had a problem believing my children, but it is easy to feel overwhelmed with so many questions being asked, and my boys would sometimes admit and sometimes deny and at times refuse to say anything at all. I took them both aside and asked questions about their father, and without hesitation they continued to accuse Andy and his family of sexual abuse. To this day, they have yet to refute what they said as children.

I will say that one good thing came out of what happened. A supervisor at the police department put in a request to have a special room made for small children to be interviewed in alleged sexual-abuse cases. Of course, she said one was already in the works; it had nothing to do with the injustice done to my children and my own outcry for a better system to be put in place for small children.

Our local television station aired the story along with personal interviews involving all three us—Heidi, Donna, and myself. They were courageous women who didn't give up and helped fight for justice against a system that greatly failed this particular group of small children, not to mention protecting others from the same fate.

The legal system failed me also. I didn't trust the authorities from the beginning, because of their failure to help me when I was raped. But after this, I wouldn't be surprised at anything. We had the support of an expert therapist and a medical doctor, and I knew my children were telling the truth as well as the other children, but it wasn't enough for the victims to see justice.

This period in my life became one of the darkest and most difficult I ever faced. For days, I couldn't move from my living-room couch. I was living a nightmare, and it never seemed to end. I felt as though heartache had followed me every day of my life, and this was all I would ever know. Even though I had failed as a wife, I never wanted to fail my children, and I felt responsible for their pain.

Looking back, there were many times my children tried to tell me. I could see their little faces looking up at me pleading and begging to stay home. But instead, I would pry their little fingers away from me and force them to stay, telling them to "be good and obey" Sara. There were warning signs of sexual abuse from the beginning, but I really didn't know what to look for.

At night I would weep as I tried to hold my two little ones and they wouldn't let me. Instead, they would scream at me and destroy their toys. One afternoon, I was desperate. I thought it would be better if I took my children and went to my mother's. My mind was running wild, and I was confused. Was Mona right? Did Bobby sexually abuse his own children? When I asked them they said no, but I didn't know what to believe.

I packed our clothes while my husband was gone, feeling that I really should leave and stay with my mother for a while, when suddenly I thought, *"Take all you can and don't come back."*

Before I could talk myself out of it, I packed the car with everything I could possibly fit into the trunk. Running from room to room, throwing clothes in plastic bags, I was begging my kids to hurry and get in the car. My children were bewildered and confused.

We drove around town while I tried to make up my mind. The Arizona sun was scorching that day. Hot and tired my kids were fighting and complaining.

I stopped at a convenience store and bought us all drinks, but I was frightened. I didn't know what to do. It had been a long time since I had made any decision on my own.

My thoughts were jumbled. *"Do I dare?"* And then, *"I can't believe I'm doing this".* Finally, I felt guilty. As a family, we were being torn apart by the repercussions of the children's abuse, and (imagine this) I felt sorry for Bobby knowing I was taking his children away from him. I had a chance. I was ready to take my three little boys with me to my mother's home in Mexico. I had a place to go, but with a heavy heart, I turned my car around and headed for home.

In the meantime, my husband had come home and found I had packed up the kids and taken them away from him. As I drove into the driveway, I saw him standing by the front door, and a sinking feeling came over me. He didn't say anything in front of the kids; he waited until he had all of us behind closed doors.

He grabbed me by the arm, and as he twisted it, he wanted to know what I was trying to pull. I told him I was just trying to do what was best for our boys, but he continued twisting my arm until I thought he would break it. He yelled at the kids to get in their room, and then he forced me into our bedroom, locking the door behind him. Then he began throwing me around the room like a rag doll.

"Where in the hell did you think you were going?" he screamed.

I tried answering him, but every time I opened my mouth, he slapped me.

"I'll kill you this time," he swore as he knocked me to the floor.

Everything happened so fast. Fending off each blow, I was terrified.

I could hear the boys screaming in the other room, but I didn't have time to think. In a heartbeat, Bobby was on top of me, hitting me like a punching bag in the ribs.

I struggled against him; screaming in bloody terror, I fought against him.

For a split second, I felt enough space to pull away from him. I scrambled to my feet. He tried grabbing hold of me, but I ran, jumping over the bed as he chased after me.

Desperately, I wanted to reach the bathroom, but he was faster than I was. He grabbed me by the neck, throwing me up against the wall. Screaming for help, I knew no one would hear me locked inside my bedroom, and I was terrified that this time I would be dead.

"Please let me go," I begged.

As I crumpled in a heap on my bedroom floor, no longer able to fight back, he stopped beating me. Then calmly, as he had done so many times before, he walked away from me.

"Don't you ever leave again with my boys," he yelled. "Get the hell out, I don't care if I ever see you again, but don't ever take my boys. If you do, I swear I'll kill you." He opened the door and left.

As soon as my children heard the closing of the front door, they came out of their rooms, obviously frightened.

"Mommy, Mommy, are you hurt?" they screamed as they ran into my room.

I didn't want them to see me. I just wanted them to leave me alone.

My body was bruised, and it was hard to breathe. I cried, but soon the sobbing stopped. Deepening despair settled in the pit of my stomach. He could have killed me.

Why did he stop?

That afternoon, he beat me worse than ever before, and for nearly a week, I could hardly get out of bed, not just from physical pain or wanting to hide my bruises—I just didn't have the will to face another day.

For weeks to come, my world was dark, darker than it had been before. I managed to get through each day as long as nothing else happened. It was enough to keep myself safe and away from an angry husband.

Now I was really angry with God. He had never answered my prayers, and I lived with that. I had been violated and raped, and I lived with that.

I had been beaten and humiliated by my husband, and I lived with that.

But I could not believe in a God who allowed terrible things to happen to children—*my* children.

I tried getting back into life again. I had a job that was important to me, but from the beginning, Bobby continually showed up at the sales office, creating scenes by fighting with me. The builder for whom I worked asked me to keep him away or he would get a restraining order against him. I wasn't able to keep Bobby away from me at the office any more than I could control his behavior at home.

One day, the owner of the subdivision handed me a piece of paper. It was a list of every broker Bobby had ever worked for, and the list was quite lengthy. The point he was trying to make was, your husband has a personality disorder and it's impossible for him to get along with other people.

My boss had also been my bishop at one time. He knew of the abuse and our welfare dependency, but that afternoon he embarrassed me in front of my coworkers by saying, "Do you know what kind of man your husband is?"

Humiliated, I answered, "I don't want to answer that here in the office."

He snatched the paper from my hand and said, "Keep him away or I'll have him arrested."

From that day on, I felt hostility from my two coworkers. To say the least, I felt inferior and shamed by what they knew of me. It seemed as though I was assigned floor duty on every holiday, and that angered Bobby.

Then one Sunday, which happened to be Mother's Day, Bobby refused to let me go to work.

That was the last straw. Everyone at the sales office was really angry with me; consequently, I let Bobby convince me I was better off quitting.

In the weeks that followed, we didn't have much of a choice. As usual, we were behind on our mortgage payments. We did find a buyer for the home, and within thirty days we had to find another place to live.

Neighbors we thought were our friends had turned their backs on us because of the sex-abuse allegations, so this time moving came as a relief. I also felt like Bobby and I were a team. Over the years, I had made up so many excuses to stay with him that I was blind to the reality of what was happening. I believed we were taking our young children away from a hostile environment to keep them safe. We were living inside a violent and hostile environment but by now I had given up hope of escaping from my abusive husband. With three small children and a failed attempt at financial independency, I felt extremely trapped and emotionally, I was beaten down.

8

My Childhood Abuse,
Part of the Cycle

Even during stormy weather, there is a moment of calmness,
but when you are a battered woman the lull ends only too soon.

Memories of cool desert air, a breeze dancing with soft flowing curtains and doves cooing in our backyard, momentarily reflected peace—we were in another home, and it still smelled of fresh paint.

Our previous neighborhood was on the other side of town. Unfriendly neighbors who talked behind our backs and taunted my children were slowly fading into the background, and I had hopes of moving forward.

I was a mother with a mission. I was doing something positive to help my children recover, and I also agreed to another television interview about the sex scandal—charges that would never be filed against the alleged sex offenders. I wanted people to know that this sort of thing happens in well-kept, middle-class neighborhoods.

The founder of the clinic where my children received counseling was a kind and loving woman. She insisted that both Bobby and I were victims of sexual abuse. I denied it. I didn't want Bobby to know what happened to me as a child. She explained to me the reasons why I was unable to cope with my children's abuse. I wasn't experiencing their pain, I was reliving my own.

Adele, impressed by my natural ability to work with victims, asked me to help her. Several hours each week I spent time in her small clinic for sexually abused children.

I seemed more in control of my life during this time—not that Bobby had changed, but something inside me had changed. I found purpose and meaning in my life, even though it came as a bittersweet gift from painful experiences. I was helping others; I was giving of myself.

Bobby and I also found a set of plans that we both fell in love with. It was our dream home, a beautiful Victorian house with stained-glass windows and a porch that wrapped around the house.

He also assumed mortgages on several duplexes that he made an income off of, and we were busy watching the house as it was built from the ground up. My boys were making friends and entering a new school.

Finally, the house was finished. We moved in without any fighting. Then one night Rob and Darinn were quietly playing in their room. They had taken a box of finger paints and spread paper out on their bedroom floor. Bobby went in to check on them. The next minute, I heard him screaming at them. I ran to the door and found him standing them against the wall.

"Who got the paint on the carpet?" he yelled.

"Bobby, please, for heaven's sake, it's a smear. I can clean it up."

He demanded that they answer him, but of course, they both denied it. They were afraid of what he would do to them.

I begged the boys, "Just tell your daddy who did it, and he won't be mad at you." I was lying and I knew it, but if they confessed earlier on, their punishment would be less severe.

It didn't matter what I said, they weren't about to accept the blame. Perhaps, neither one of them really knew who spilled the paint. I ran into the kitchen to grab some cleaning supplies while Bobby was still screaming at the kids. I was on the floor scrubbing, and they were up against the wall being yelled at. Disgusted that neither one would answer him, he took off his belt.

I knew they were in for it. Bobby started whipping them repeatedly, because now he had a liar to punish as well as the perpetrator of the initial crime. As I said before, Bobby hated liars, and everyone except him was always a liar.

My two little boys were jumping around the room screaming as the belt hit their legs, and I was screaming at Bobby to stop. Darinn was completely knocked off his feet; the belt hit him so hard. Then he screamed, "I did it, Daddy, I was the one that did it."

Bobby wasn't about to believe him. Instead, he said they were both liars.

The more I begged him to stop, the angrier he became. I ran in front of his belt to stop him, but he turned the belt on me. I was hysterical trying to protect them while at the same time trying to fend off that vicious belt.

I screamed at the kids to stop running. "Stand still," I screamed, "and then he won't hit you as hard." But they wouldn't stop running, and Bobby hit them across their backs.

Once the crisis was over, my two little boys and I huddled together on the floor crying and comforting each other.

Over and over my children said, "I'm sorry for lying, Mommy."

The boys were afraid of their dad, even before he beat them. If he played too rough and they complained, he got angry. They had to tiptoe around him and stay out of his way so as not to make him angry. Not only did I have to learn how to obey the rules, now I had to teach my children.

Several years after filing suit against our insurance company for breech of contract once they failed to cover the car that went into the lake, our long-awaited court date finally arrived. The trial lasted about two weeks. Once it was over and the jury was in deliberation, we waited.

The following day, we received word that they had received a decision. I was apprehensive. What if we lost? I just knew Bobby would fly off the handle and scream at everyone inside the courthouse, and I didn't want to be there. So I faked an excruciating headache. I regretted it once Bobby returned home and said that the jury awarded us a large settlement. Of course, our insurance company appealed, but at least it was over.

Several months later, we reached an agreement with our insurance company, and with the small amount we received, Bobby bought himself a pickup. I put what was left aside to open a small business, knowing that if I didn't invest what money we had into some kind of business, I would never have stability in my life.

Nathan, my fourth son, was born on July 20, 1987. He was to have been my girl. As soon as I learned I was pregnant, I felt sure I would give birth to the daughter I longed for. In no time, I had drawers filled with pink outfits—but I had a sonogram just before he was born, and so I knew I was having another boy.

My heart was so set on a little girl that at first, I was disappointed. But I don't know how any mother feels the least bit of disappointment when the baby is born and she holds him in her arms. No matter what Bobby had done to me, there was still a mother's love he could never touch.

Robby and Darinn were in school, and Justin spent most of his time with his father. Bobby would bring him home, after being gone all day, loaded with toys. The other boys were so jealous. I asked

Bobby to treat them equally, but he never listened. First he spoiled Robby, ignoring Darinn, and now he took up with Justin where he left off with Robby.

Bobby and I decided to open a country store. We went on buying trips. Our life together seemed to change for a while, and one of my most memorable experiences with Bobby was the week we spent in Pennsylvania.

We were there during the fall. Never had I seen such brilliant autumn colors—leaves falling in brisk air covering the ground with a blanket of orange, red, and yellow hues. Candles shining in neighborhood windows welcomed passing strangers, and seas of green covering rolling hills painted an intriguing scene.

The countryside was breathtaking, and each row of clotheslines with hanging Amish quilts captivated the eye as far as you could see—they were unending from farm to farm. Renewed by wisps of flickering hope, I fervently prayed for lasting memories of happier days.

Over the following months, I was so involved with the business; it became part of my life. Wholesale gift shows were held in California, and we would drive there, stay the night, attend the show, and come home. I was creative, and what I didn't purchase, I made.

Bobby was a skilled craftsman. He made beautiful furniture, mostly primitive or Amish style, and we added that to our shop. I found a part of myself that was missing in the midst of painting walls, putting up wallpaper, and creating wreaths, dolls, and other homemade items.

My store was more than just a part of me; it was almost like a child that slipped quietly into my life. She was graceful joy; a gift from God renewing my faith in the goodness life had to offer.

Mornings had changed. I didn't dread facing the day. Instead, I looked forward to unlocking the front door, smelling fragrant spices, and becoming lost in another world.

My store was as much a part of me as each breath I took. I saw it as my last resort; it would either be a success or a complete failure that would be devastating.

With in a year and a half, I was pregnant again. But this time it was different. I was happier. There was less stress, and Bobby was less violent.

Every morning I went to work and stayed long after closing hours painting, sewing, or creating floral arrangements. I did everything I could, not only for my business, but to stay away from home.

I would close my shop long enough to pick the kids up from school and then return to finish working. Even today, somewhere in my memories, my little blue house on Main Street still exists and I'm heavy with child, rocking back and forth in an old chair, greeting my customers and loving the smells.

On Saturdays, Rob, Darinn, and Justin worked with me. They mowed the lawn and cleaned out my craft room. They even loved to sit at the counter and help me make sales.

At the end of the week I would pay them, and out the front door they would run, heading straight for Dairy Queen. Before they returned, most of their money had been spent.

This was living. This was joy. Watching my children laugh and work together filled my soul with thanksgiving, and then I softly whispered, *Thank you God for giving me another chance.*

One afternoon, I was at the doctor's office and the nurse did an ultrasound. My doctor's staff knew how badly I wanted a girl. That afternoon, the nurse jubilantly exclaimed that this baby was indeed a girl. Quickly she showed me on the monitor just what she was seeing.

I was elated. There on the screen was proof I was carrying a girl. After four boys, I had almost given up hope. Rapidly, that very afternoon, I was planning my daughter's life. She would never grow up to be like me!

A sister in our ward, Judy, often cared for Nathan. When I was exhausted, this sweet lady came over and took Nathan home with her. She was a mother to me and an angel to my baby son. Inside her safe home, she held him and loved him as though he was one of her own. Even though my life is not one I would wish on anyone, I have been blessed with Earth-angels who came into my life when I needed them. God bless them wherever they are today.

Inevitably, things began to change. We weren't doing as well. Several of the duplexes Bobby owned were foreclosed. Our business struggled to keep up with its expenses.

Lynsey was born on February 28, 1988. A few days later, I brought her home from the hospital and carried her up the staircase into her bedroom. White lacy curtains kept the sun away. Pink wallpaper with tiny teddy bears lined her walls, giving the room a delicate nursery touch. But her days, as well as mine, were limited in my beloved home.

My baby girl was the center of my life. I dressed her in everything pink, from socks to clothing to warm comfy blankets, including the little bows stuck in her hair with honey.

She was beautiful as a baby, and she still is.

Lynsey has a mind of her own and always has. Sometimes, I feel cursed because of this, and then I remember how I used to be. That's when I encourage her to be herself. I don't ever want to take away her individuality and right to be loved and treated with respect.

9

Physically, Emotionally Battered
and Severe Depression

*I didn't listen to my heart, but I couldn't deny dreams fading
as they were washed away along the shores of anguish.*

It wasn't long before Bobby no longer had any one of his apartment complexes—they had all been foreclosed, and we were without an income. It did bother me, though, that many of his renters couldn't afford to find another place to live once the bank gave them an eviction notice without refunding their deposits.

The day came all too soon when we had to pack everything that belonged to us; it was time to say good-bye to another place I had called home. I remember those days all too well, because I remember packing a zillion boxes and hating the life I had been living. I threw stuff into boxes so unorganized that many things were broken, but I didn't care. I didn't even want to take them with me. I was angry, tired, and resentful—not enough to divorce my husband, but I hated him enough to wish him dead.

Once I had enough boxes packed, I brought them to the garage and loaded them into the old blue station wagon that my mother had purchased for me. Where was Bobby? I didn't know and I didn't care.

I had to say good-bye to my home—each tear that fell washed away another hope and another dream. I had a right to cry, and I didn't want him to see my tears. They were sacred to me, and they gave meaning to something I had forgotten—to honor my feelings.

Slowly, I made my way back into the house, mesmerized by the flowers I had just planted. They were blooming, and my vines were sprouting new growth. Old orange trees shaded the front porch; they were always my favorite, and that day fragrant breezes danced with my pink ruffled curtains. Breathing in the air around me, I stumbled against the stairs, unable to see past an ocean of tears. I stayed there for a moment, and then I slowly entered the house, making my way into my bathroom with another box that needed to be filled.

I paused from packing to gaze out my bathroom window. Watching the birds gather around a feeder I had hanging, I envied those little feathery friends. They never had to worry about someone taking their home away from them.

As for me, this was my life story. Sadness, deeper than I had ever felt before, seeped into my heart, like warm running water, threatening to drown me in sorrow.

Bobby had made arrangements with an owner to purchase a house that was just around the corner from our beautiful home that was in foreclosure. He gave the man a small deposit, and they both signed the contract. I hated deceiving others. I knew that Bobby wouldn't pay the owner when the first payment was due—but Bobby knew, because of the purchase agreement, that we would have several months before the owner could have us evicted.

Later, I spoke to our bishop concerning our need for welfare assistance. In his office, I cried. I said I couldn't do it anymore. I was tired of being a wife who felt like she needed to "endure to the end."

I tried to make him understand the dire circumstances in our home, not only financially but also emotionally. In desperation, I entrusted him with my soul, praying he would have the answer I needed when I told him, "My husband is abusive, and he is destroying our family."

The only reply he had was a two-part question: Was I conducting family home-evenings every Monday night, and was I paying my tithing? Because, he said, if I would always remember to do that, our family would receive the blessings from our obedience.

He also knew that Bobby and I had not been attending the temple like we should. "Go home," he said, "and think about the things you should be doing, and maybe you will realize a greater need to be faithful to the instructions received from the first presidency of the church."

I left that office feeling hopeless. I had gone there hoping the bishop would chastise my husband, call him to repentance, or force him into counseling. Instead, I felt more burdened with guilt. What more could I possibly do?

Everything around me appeared to be dark and gloomy. As days went by, I didn't want to get out of bed. But my children needed me and so did my store—somehow I made myself do what my heart no longer believed in doing, even though I desperately wanted to give up.

Bobby wasn't working in real estate or any other type of job. My store barely kept up with its own financial obligations. It just wasn't possible to support our needs at home also. I begged Bobby to find a job until we built the business up. He wouldn't hear of it. The store, he said, was his. It was paid for with his money (I never figured that one out), and I was running it into the ground. Since there wasn't enough money to support our household expenses and the store's expenses, I had to be doing something wrong. Bobby decided I had to stay home, where I couldn't mess things up any worse than I already had, and he would run the business.

At home, the days were long, and I felt lifeless. Some days I hardly left my bed. Sometimes I fixed breakfast for the kids, and sometimes I didn't. I longed to be back at my store; it was all I had left.

Then I found out I was pregnant. What was I thinking? Or was I thinking at all? How could I possibly bring another baby into this family? Lynsey wasn't even a year old when I found out I would be having another baby. I don't really remember caring for her at times. Perhaps she stayed covered up in bed with me.

Where was Nathan? Maybe he quietly played in his bedroom, afraid to make any noise, fearing that he might wake the mean and nasty dragon that I had become. I didn't have the strength to care for my children. Instead, I wanted to stop breathing and softly fade away, just like nighttime shadows dancing on the wall disappear in early morning light.

Bobby arrived home late one evening and walked into a dirty kitchen. The sink was filled with every dish we owned. The laundry-room floor was covered with dirty clothes. I waited for him to start yelling—this time, I don't know that I even cared. That is, until Bobby started throwing things around in the kitchen, yelling loud enough for the neighborhood to hear.

His frustration was all about me. He said out loud to himself that he had to do everything. Since I couldn't clean house or fix a decent meal, he was going to Kentucky Fried Chicken to get something for the kids to eat.

He returned with an armful of boxes. He opened each one and put food on their plates. I came into the kitchen to make sure the kids were okay. The minute I saw him open up a container with coleslaw, I started to say, "Don't give that to Darinn," but I was too late. Bobby had already heaped a ton of coleslaw onto his plate. Darinn hated coleslaw, and I knew that a war was about to start.

Silently, I prayed, *"Darinn, just eat it."*

Instead, the first thing he said was, "Dad, why did you give me coleslaw when you know I hate it?"

Oh boy, lightning was about to hit.

My boys never learned. They were supposed to do things they didn't want to do and say things they didn't want to say to save the family peace. But Darinn wasn't about to cooperate; he never did when he felt that he was in the right.

Bobby lost his patience, grabbed the spoon, and started shoving the coleslaw into his mouth. Darinn was gagging with each spoonful, and Bobby only shoveled it in faster.

I begged Bobby to slow down and let him do it himself. He warned me to stay out of it.

Then Darinn started crying. Between sniffling and tears, his dad forced one spoonful after another until suddenly he vomited all over his plate.

Without missing a beat, Bobby scooped up the coleslaw mixed with vomit and continued forcing it down his throat.

I grabbed Bobby by the hand and told him to stop his madness. Bobby threw me against the kitchen wall. Pictures and glass plates came crashing to the floor as Bobby smashed my head against the wall.

The kids were screaming, "Dad, stop it, you're hurting Mom."

Each time he hit my head against the wall, I saw stars. My head was pounding. I tried to push him off, but he kneed me in the stomach, knocking the breath out of me. Darinn got up from the table trying to pull Bobby off me, screaming, "I'll eat it, Dad. I promise I'll eat it. Just let go of Mom."

Bobby let go of me and told me to go back to bed.

He ordered the kids to get back to the table and for everyone to shut up. Then he told the kids, "See what your mom causes every time?

Clothes were piled everywhere, even in my bedroom, and I could hardly find my way to bed. Bobby came inside the doorway and said that if I didn't straighten up he was going to call Child Protective Services and have the children taken away from me. I had ruined him financially, and I was nothing more than a burden to him.

I couldn't stop sobbing. I begged Bobby to leave me alone. I was sick, I told him.

"You're sick all right," he screamed back at me. "And I'm sick of putting up with you."

"You don't understand, Bobby. I really need help. I'm afraid I'm going to die."

"Good," he said. "Save me from doing it for you."

We were forced to move again after six months because we failed to make any payments to the owner. Bobby found a house across town. He took money from the business to pay the rent; so consequently, we were behind on our business lease.

Bobby and I packed all our belongings again, and I think the only lesson I learned was that I should have kept everything in boxes from the last move. We never stayed in any house long enough to make unpacking worthwhile.

My boys enrolled in yet another school. This time, Robby's teacher called me in for a parent/teacher conference. She said Robby had difficulties in class, and she wanted him tested. He was eight years old and in the third grade. He had struggled since kindergarten, and even though other teachers had mentioned a learning disability, nothing was ever really done about it. I had taken Robby for tutoring, but he wasn't able to keep up with his class.

Over the following year, I felt extremely frustrated with the education system. Robby didn't qualify for any educational program. In time, I felt pressured into placing him in the educable mentally handicapped children's program. Since he really didn't fit the requirements for that program, I refused to enroll him. Consequently, Rob stayed within the mainstream while being completely unable to keep up with the other kids.

As Robby grew older, he shut out the world. He had moved from too many neighborhoods and grade schools. Robby had a tender heart that had been shattered, and he would never let anyone get close to him. Then a woman in our ward told me about someone who had a private school.

When I met Belle, she diligently worked with Robby. She had a way with broken hearts, and she knew how to reach those who had emotionally shut down. She had devoted her life to helping students achieve to the best of their own ability, and I know she made a difference in my son's life. Even though our resources were limited, Belle never turned anyone away because they couldn't pay for her services.

Small, healthy changes were taking place within Rob. He spent his days at Belle's learning center, and he played baseball in the evenings. He was naturally gifted as the team pitcher. Bobby volunteered to coach the team one year, and this is how he knew that a team of professional ballplayers was touring the country looking for talented young players for the Young American Ambassadors. Those who made the team would have the opportunity to play against teams in foreign countries. Bobby told Robby he had to try out.

I remember the day I took Robby to the ballpark for tryouts. "Mom," he said, "I'll never be good enough to make the team."

I promised him that if he did his very best, he would be proud of his courage, and that would be enough. Gallantly, he held on to his glove as he walked toward a group of people he had never met before. My heart ached seeing this small young boy—who, at ten years of age, had faced more challenges in his life than I ever knew existed— walk across the field, but I was also extremely proud of him.

A few weeks later, he received an official letter in the mail from the American Ambassadors. He ripped open the envelope. The instant he read it, he started jumping up and down shouting, "I made the team, Mom!" He kept repeating those words, unable to believe something good had actually happened in his life. I was as excited and happy for him as he was.

As I read the letter, my heart sank. He would need several thousand dollars, and we just didn't have it. I had to wonder if Bobby had known it would take money before he encouraged Rob to try out. I asked my husband why he didn't tell us about the cost.

He answered me saying, "I just wanted to see if he could make the team."

Bobby wouldn't tell Robby, so I had to tell him that he couldn't go. The disappointment on his face transcends any word in my vocabulary, but my heart still felt his pain. To this day, Rob has never forgotten that he made the team; he talks about it often, wishing that if his life had been different he could have realized his dreams.

Bobby had been working at the shop for quite some time while I stayed at home. One day, a delivery truck showed up at my door. The driver told me my husband had sent him to pick up a check for a delivery he had made at the store. Quickly, I called Bobby, and he instructed me that I was to make out two postdated checks, explaining that he knew what he was doing.

"Why do you want me to sign the checks?" I asked.

He said he had run out of checks at the store and knew I had extra business checks at home.

Just to make sure, I called the company long-distance and talked to their bookkeeper. She said Bobby had made prior arrangements with the owner, and the owner would accept two postdated checks exactly fifteen days apart.

I called Bobby and said, "I can't do this. We can't afford to carry inventory like that and pay for it in less than thirty days."

Bobby assured me he had a customer who had placed an order for the furniture, and he would deposit the money as soon as he made the delivery.

Reluctantly, I signed the checks and gave them to the driver, and he left. I walked back inside the kitchen with a sinking feeling that I had just done something I would regret.

When the time came, Bobby didn't deliver the furniture like he said he would. When I questioned him about it, he was irritated and told me, "The furniture isn't worth a dime, and I can't sell it." He went on to say that he had never seen such sloppy craftsmanship, and I was to send the furniture back.

I was furious. I couldn't just send back an entire truckload of furniture. Knowing Bobby had to been deceitful about having the furniture previously sold, I called the owner and explained that we weren't satisfied with the furniture he had shipped. The owner was polite and said he would send a truck within a few weeks from California. I explained that I would have to place a stop payment on the checks since I didn't have sufficient funds to cover the amounts. He said okay.

On the day the truck was to arrive, Bobby said he would open the store and help the driver load the furniture. So I stayed home.

Within a few hours, I received a call from Bobby. He said the police were at the shop.

"Why?" I asked.

He told me he didn't like the attitude of the truck driver and wasn't about to let him on the property. The truck driver called the police for assistance, but they, without a court order, could not force Bobby to open the doors.

Panicked, I begged Bobby, "For heaven's sake, please let the driver take the furniture. I gave the owner my word. I've already put a stop payment on the checks. You can't do this."

He hung up the phone on me, and I didn't have a way to get to the store to do anything about it. I had the owner's phone number, so I called him and apologized. I said it was a misunderstanding and to please send the driver back and I would see to it he received his furniture.

The truck driver returned. Again, Bobby refused to let him on the property. The truck driver left, and when I called the owner several days later, he was furious. He said they only made deliveries in Arizona and California a few times a year. It would take him a while before his driver would be in our area.

I stayed at the store full-time from then on, and Bobby stayed at home. He continued to build built country pine furniture. There was a demand for what he made; he just couldn't keep up with the orders.

My life as I had known it with Bobby was slowly coming to end. As I look back, it had to have been fate forcing a breakthrough, as if everything had run its course.

Mesa is famous for having holiday boutiques. Mormon women who got together to sell their handmade crafts held these boutiques in homes. It started out as something small and insignificant, but it became a booming business, especially during peak seasons for business owners. Consequently, gift shops like mine suffered.

That same year, July of 1989, Westin was born. In twelve years, I had given birth to six children, and I loved them dearly, but this was not the way I had planned my life or theirs. This time, I stayed at my mother's in Mexico until Westin was born. Several weeks later, I took him home. Severely depressed and without sleep, I was extremely tired getting up at night, fixing his bottle, feeding him, and waiting until he went back to sleep.

One night, I placed him on the kitchen counter right next to me while I mixed his formula. I had been without sleep for days, and I wasn't thinking. Everything seemed to be in slow motion. I turned for just a second and the baby fell. He landed on the hard tile floor. I grabbed him and picked him up from the floor while he was really crying.

Running into the bathroom, I quickly closed the door. The last thing I wanted was to wake Bobby up. Sobbing, I held my baby, and I stayed in the bathroom most of the night—praying that he would be okay. The moment he closed his eyes I would wake him, fearing what I might have done.

I felt the arms of all my children reaching out to me at the same time, crying and begging for me to save them. Panicked, I wanted to run. They needed something more than I could offer them. I had lived too many years without a moment of peace and too many years of chronic abuse and severe depression. I was so sick of living.

Somehow I made it through the first few months after giving birth to Westin, but then late one night as I held my newborn baby, a memory of long ago filled my heart.

I was in a cold room staring up at the lights.

Someone was saying, "It will soon be over." I was ending my unborn baby's life. I could not stop the hands of time from taking me back. Grief washed over me as though I had suddenly suffered a profound death—a loss so great I could not bear the pain.

Back and forth I rocked Westin, unable to stop the tears. The life I had once ended by having an abortion still remained with me after all the years that had passed. Is this how a mother is to be punished when she takes away the life of her unborn child? I hurt so deeply, I felt grief fill every pore of my body as though I was bleeding.

The choices I had made, first as a young woman and then as a mother, filled my heart with sorrow. I knew that every child to whom I gave birth was to have made up for the one I did not. Was I ever to be forgiven? As I watched my sleeping baby, I wanted to turn back the hands of time. Life would have been so different had I made different choices.

I felt suffocated in the life I had created; I could feel my time was running out. I didn't have the emotional stability to care for this baby, and I knew it. My other children struggled in school, and I felt drained of the strength I needed to function as a mother.

Bobby and I were forced to move again. We couldn't pay our rent. We stayed beyond our thirty days, but that gave us time to come up with enough money to move into something else. Bobby found a house just around the corner. It was an older house, one that had a barn and a huge backyard. To the side was a garden filled with grapevines.

"*Yes,*" I thought to myself, "*I can turn this one into a home.*"

Bobby told me he had worked out another deal with the owner—the house didn't have a mortgage. We could live there and pay the owners rent until we found suitable financing. And so, once again, in late 1989, we packed our belongings. This time, my children were old enough to help. I felt like we were a family of tiny waifs, ungrounded and wounded. But they were also excited. No one liked the house we'd been living in. It didn't have enough windows to let the sunshine in. It was old and needed repairs, and it never felt like home.

We moved in the fall, and leaves had covered the yard. For a while, I remember laughter as Nate and Lynsey played in piles of leaves.

We lived in this house for one year, struggling between keeping our doors open to our business and a roof over our heads. Soon we were behind on our mortgage payments. I went to our bishop and asked for help. Our bishop, being concerned, agreed to help us with rent, utilities, and food. After paying our bills for six months, he insisted that Bobby find suitable employment.

"With my education," he adamantly said, "I will never lower myself to work for minimum wages."

"But you aren't making any money at what you are doing," was the bishop's reply.

Bobby was insulted, and his relationship with the bishop was severely strained.

The bishop called me one morning to suggest I convince Bobby he should take any job he could find.

"He has an awful temper, and I can't talk to him," he said.

Tears quickly sprang to my eyes, and it was all I could do to choke back the tears. "I know, Bishop," I said. "This is what I've been trying to tell you."

"Well," he said, "I don't know how I can help you, but I can't allow you to receive welfare assistance under the circumstances."

Placing the receiver into its cradle, I fell into a heap on the floor. Sobbing, I had never felt such distress. I had always been trained to ask my church leaders for help. I wasn't to go outside my faith for anything. The outside world would only lead me astray, because they didn't understand our family values.

It wasn't long before the doors to my shop closed for good, and my dream died with it. I had a "going out of business sale," and each day spent in my store brought heartache deeper than any other.

Frantically, Bobby tried to find a way out of the mess we were in. He found that solution one morning when my mother called to see how I was doing. Bobby told her I was really depressed because we were losing our home. I would have never gone to my mother to ask her for a dime, but Bobby did, and my mother sent us the money to catch up on our house payments.

One day, Bobby had another idea. He had always told me that, years before we met, he had graduated from Arizona State University. His diploma was hanging on our wall. He wanted to go back to ASU and get his teaching certificate. He said it would only take him two semesters, as he had already graduated from ASU, and I was desperate enough to believe him. He also asked my mother to continue helping us while he got through one year of school.

For the first time, I felt a glimmer of hope. A teaching job would offer consistent income, one I had never had with Bobby.

That fall, Bobby enrolled in classes at Arizona State University, and school had also started for my children. But even with hope for a better way of living, I was severely depressed, and it was difficult to get out of bed each morning. I couldn't put one foot in front of the other without falling apart; fear was the only motivator that forced me to do it. Bobby couldn't tolerate it when I was sick. Terrified of his temper, each morning I forced myself to get up and fix breakfast, but I didn't do it without crying, and I don't remember taking a shower before I dressed or taking care of myself.

The boys were older now, and they had friends over. One evening, they built a skate ramp in front of our house. They made a mess with boards lying in the street. Bobby drove up, jumped out of his pickup, and started swearing at the boys. Hearing Bobby yell, I ran outside to the carport. Helplessly I listened as he demanded they clean it up. He threw boards at all of them, but in throwing boards, nails, and tools he only fueled his rage until he had completely broken apart their skate ramp.

I felt my heart twist in agony for my boys. They were so embarrassed and humiliated in front of their friends. I tried to stop him, but he yelled at me for allowing them to make our street look like a place "where white trash lived."

I felt like saying, "*That's exactly what we are, white trash, because you've made us look like that.*" Rob and Darinn's friends ran from our house that day and didn't come over again.

Over the following months, it seemed to be worse for my boys. Bobby wasn't using me as his whipping post. He was after his children, and they were forever getting into trouble. Rob threw a baseball and it shattered the bathroom window. He ran. He hid in the barn for several hours, and Bobby couldn't find him. Later on,

Darinn accidentally broke Bobby's jar of precious antique marbles. He was whipped for that mistake.

Early in the mornings, Bobby delivered newspapers. He would leave the house around four a.m., and he always forced the boys to go with him. They hated to go. Bobby yelled at them each time they did any little thing wrong, such as not folding fast enough or throwing the paper in the wrong place.

Whenever I needed my husband to take over, he became angry. Instead of helping me, he would shame me for my mental state.

"You're really crazy," he would say and warn the children to stay away from me.

Many times when he reduced me to a whimpering child, he would remind the kids what he had to put up with. "Look at your mother," he would say. "She's really crazy, isn't she?"

Often he would drag me by my hair, forcing me to see clothes that were piling up and garbage that hadn't been disposed of. Because it wasn't his job to help me clean the house, the house remained unkempt; the children had been fixing their own meals and digging through dirty piles of laundry to find a shirt or a pair of socks. Even though I tried, I just couldn't force myself out of bed.

One morning I did get out of bed through sheer force of will, feeling extreme anxiety because I knew Bobby was at his breaking point. I walked into the living room before the children left for school, and he began cursing me for the mess our lives were in.

That's when the hitting began. The kids begged him to stop, but he wouldn't listen. Instead, he grabbed a hall tree standing in the corner and began beating me over the back with it. The kids screamed as I fell to the floor and he continued to beat me.

No matter how hard my children tried, they couldn't make him stop. Finally he shouted, "You're not even worth wasting my time."

Only then did he walk away. Once he did, my children helped me into my bedroom. The pain was so great it felt as though he had broken a rib. I had bruises all over my body, and there was no way my children could leave for school. Instead, they climbed into bed with me and promised they would behave if I would only get better.

Most of my life, I had wanted nothing more than to be a mother, but never once did I imagine my life would turn out the way it did. I was severely depressed, unable to cope with anything. Unable to shut out the pain, often I screamed in terror, knowing my mind was slipping away into outer darkness and would never return.

I would find myself in my closet. Perhaps I found refuge in the darkness; perhaps I thought I could lie down and die; perhaps there just wasn't any other place left to go. I still remember my children begging me to stop crying and come out. They would find me huddled in a corner, sobbing uncontrollably.

One afternoon, I made my way into the living room and opened the Yellow Pages. I needed to find a doctor. I found a general practitioner whose office was close by and dialed his number. The moment his receptionist answered, I hung up.

"What will I say to them?"

I dialed several times before I stayed on the line and said, "I need help." An appointment was made for that afternoon, and I was nervous about going. Making that first call to a doctor took incredible strength.

Dr. Stevens had some blood work done, and later we talked. He explained why I felt so despondent and was unable to function. I suffered from depression. I cried a flood of tears when he said I wasn't crazy or weak, but that I had an illness. He said many people suffer from the same disorder, but there was help. His voice was gentle and comforting.

He prescribed an antidepressant and said it would take several weeks before I would feel a difference. Soon after my first appointment with Dr. Stevens, there was a knock at my door. I opened it to find two policemen on the other side. I asked them what they wanted, and they said they needed to talk to me. A complaint had been filed with the county attorney. I was being accused of fraud—those two checks I had placed a stop payment on were both staring me in the face. I answered questions that afternoon, and I knew more were soon to follow.

Within a week or so, I was given a court order to turn over all my business records, and an audit was being done on my banking transactions. This was not what I needed at the time—perhaps this was going to be the straw that broke the camel's back. I could hardly make it through interviews, until finally I sought legal counsel. I explained to an attorney what my husband had done. I didn't intentionally defraud anyone, but I don't think the county attorney or the owner of the furniture really cared to listen to my excuses. They were going after me.

I asked my attorney to find a way to settle the charges, and I would agree to make monthly payments until it was paid in full. I then used the money my mom had sent for our mortgage payments to pay my attorney.

Finally, an agreement was reached. I was to make monthly payments in the amount of $600 until the debt was satisfied. I had absolutely no idea how I was going to do that. We didn't have any income. Bobby was a full-time student, and I wasn't working until I felt forced into finding a part-time job. A neighbor knew that I was looking for work; he had me work in his office for five hours a day, but I couldn't handle it. Sometimes I couldn't get dressed, much less leave the house.

If I thought life couldn't get any worse than that, I was wrong.

Not too long after that incident, late in the evening, I was in the bedroom when my son ran into the room whispering, "Mom, there are cops all over the place; they are even in the backyard."

I jumped to my feet just as the front doorbell rang. Rushing to the door, I answered it. They had an arrest warrant—for me.

Apparently, I had written a check for $800 on a closed account for merchandise received at my business.

I denied it. I had never written a check on a closed account. The police officers were not in possession of the check, but they said I had signed it. They were to take me into custody and then extradite me to the state in which the check was received. My heart was pounding. I could hardly breathe. I kept on saying there must be some mistake

Bobby came strolling into the kitchen with a look of surprise on his face. He wanted to know what all the commotion was about. The police officer explained to him what they were about to do. My husband said since it didn't involve him, he would go back and watch TV.

With tears in my eyes and six children hanging on my waist, thank heaven the supervisor took pity on me.

He made several phone calls and then said to me, "Since you don't appear to be a flight risk, I've been given permission to let you stay here tonight. By tomorrow, you will need to contact the person to whom you gave the check and make arrangements to pay it."

He took me aside and said, "The signature on the check isn't really legible, but since only your name appears on the closed account, charges were brought against you."

The following morning, my neighbor, who was also an attorney, stopped by and said he saw all the police cars at my house the night before. He wanted to know what he could do to help. I explained the situation, and he said he would make the phone call for me.

Later that afternoon, he called me and said that all charges would be dropped if I had a certified check to him in the amount of $800 before five p.m. Once again, I took my mother's money she had sent for our mortgage payment. The other money I owed would have to wait; I was putting out one fire at a time.

It didn't take more than several weeks before my neighbor called me from his office and said he had received the check I allegedly had written. He said, "You need to take a look at this."

I hung the phone up and turned around to see Bobby standing in back of me. Meekly he said, "I need to tell you something." Hesitating, he continued, "I've been thinking about that check they said you wrote, and I sort of remember receiving an order in that amount at the shop. I paid for it, but how was I to know that account had been closed?"

He must have thought I was brain dead. Why did he forge my name at the bottom of the check? I called my neighbor at his office and told him it wouldn't be necessary to see the check, Bobby was the one who signed my name, and he said, "I know."

The following day, Bobby demanded I get off my bed long enough to call the administration office at Arizona State University. He needed to know if his financial aid check had arrived so he could pick it up. I made the phone call for him. The voice on the other end said she could not give me the information I needed; it was confidential. I begged her to tell me. She must have sensed some urgency or reason to tell me what she did, because she finally agreed that if I could identify myself as Bobby's wife, she would release the information. She asked me questions about Bobby, and I knew all the answers except one. I told her Bobby had graduated from ASU, and she said I was wrong.

"How could I be," I asked her, "when I have his degree hanging on my wall?" I insisted she must be mistaken.

She quietly answered me, "I'm not mistaken. Your husband enrolled as a freshman just this semester."

As I hung up the phone I thought, *"And he will never live long enough to finish."*

Shocked beyond belief, I waited for Bobby to walk through the front door. If I had a machine gun, even a small handgun would have worked, I would have killed him. But a good Christian woman doesn't kill her husband; therefore, I thought I would give him a chance to explain why he lied. Then I thought of my mother, my dear sweet trusting mother, doing all she could to help me because I wouldn't leave my lying, deceitful, abusive husband.

Bobby returned home that afternoon. The first thing he wanted to know was if I had the information he wanted from ASU.

"I got more than I wanted from the admissions office," I said, and then I asked him to explain to me how he got a bogus diploma from ASU when he had never graduated. He walked up to me as though he was going to slap my silly face for accusing him of something so ridiculous as lying. "Don't lie to me anymore, Bobby. I know the truth, and there is nothing you can say that will convince me to ever believe in you again."

He mumbled something like I had no right to get into his affairs and walked out of the room.

I wasn't angry with Bobby so much as I was devastated at the awful truth. How was I going to tell my mother? I had lied to her about everything. The money she sent for the house payment, I used to keep me out of jail, and we were still losing our home. I had been such a fool. Even though Bobby had betrayed me, I had betrayed my mother's trust.

10

Making a Plan of Escape

Be a lantern unto my feet. Guide me to a place where I'll be safe.
Bring comfort to a frightened heart I prayed,
and in the still of the night God answered me.

One afternoon, I remember hearing the front door open, and I panicked. I grabbed my blanket and hid in the closet. It was dark inside as I huddled against the corner. I heard footsteps coming closer, and I began to scream many times, "Please don't hurt me, Bobby."

The closet door opened and through streams of sunlight I saw Bobby standing there. Then he began to laugh. He told me I really was crazy, and he slammed the door shut again. He yelled at the kids to come and see what he had found hiding inside his closet—a demented fool.

He made fun of me as the kids were forced to watch. "This is your mother, kids," he laughed. "She is the one who is crazy. Look at her curled up like a baby crying her heart out, doesn't she make you sick? It's because of her we are losing our home." He slammed the door shut once again as I sobbed, knowing I really was crazy. I could hear him tell the kids about all the medication I was taking and how it was only making me worse.

At night I would write letters to my children begging their forgiveness, and then I would seal them and print their names on the envelopes. I wrote a letter to my mother, begging her to take care of my children if something happened to me and to take them away from their father.

A few days later, Darinn came into the living room where I was sleeping. He woke me up and said, "Mom, I need to talk to you." It seemed overnight that this little boy had grown like a weed. He was eleven and seemed to grow out of his clothes before he wore them. For days he had been complaining about not having anything to wear. Even though he was younger than Robby, he was much taller, so he couldn't share clothes with his brother. I knew what he wanted before he asked, but unable to cope with anything, I answered, "Not now, Darinn, ask me later."

Darinn said, "You always say later, Mom, but you never listen to me." With tears in his eyes he said, "My tennis shoes have holes in them. I'm embarrassed to wear them to school. Can't I please get a new pair?"

My mind flew into a panic. He was asking something of me, and I couldn't think. I didn't have any money, and I didn't have an answer for him. I started to cry. Sobbing with my head in my hands, I screamed without stopping. Bobby came running into the room holding his weight belt, demanding to know what in the hell was going on. Darinn ran into his room and tried to lock his door. Bobby beat him to it.

I stopped crying when the sounds coming from the bedroom terrified me. I could hear both my sons screaming bloody murder as Bobby hit them with his weight belt. Over and over, he whipped them. Darinn jumped on top of their bunk beds. Robby wouldn't move. He stood there while Bobby ripped welts into his skin. Tears were running down his face while he held his fists tightly against his sides.

"For God's sake, Bobby, you're going to kill him," I screamed as I put my hands up to my mouth. Bobby wouldn't stop. He grabbed Darinn from the bed, threw him to the ground, and beat him with that horrid belt.

Knowing I had to do something, I ran in front of the belt to stop him. He threw me back and told me to get out of the room. I ran toward him again and screamed, "Beat me, Bobby, but leave my boys alone."

Bobby whirled around and let me have it. I have never felt anything burn like the sting of that belt. I thought I had experienced physical pain before, but nothing hurt like that did. He raised his hand to swing one more time and the boys tried to stop him. I ran from the room into the kitchen. I ripped the buttons from my nightgown and dug my nails into my skin.

"I want to die!" I screamed. I don't know that I felt coherent. I don't know that my mind didn't snap, but I was at the end of my rope.

Bobby stopped beating his wounded boys, leaving them in their room crying, and then he pushed me aside, yelling that this was my fault.

"You're a pathetic bitch," he said. He stormed down the hallway ranting, "You have done this to your kids," and he slammed his bedroom door.

That night, in my wild and crazy head, the walls of denial shattered releasing my anguished pain. There was nothing left to live for.

I emptied my cupboard and took out pills of every kind. Bobby had access to painkillers, and he had enough. Whatever medication was in there, I took it and swallowed a handful at a time.

I made my way to the living room, lay down on the couch, and pulled a quilt over me. Peace filling my being. I believed the pain would now stop.

I wouldn't hurt anymore.

I listened to my boys crying, and my heart shattered into a million tiny pieces. Then my world fell silent.

I don't know when, but Darinn found the empty pill containers spread all over the kitchen counter, and the next thing I remember was my son screaming at me and trying to make me get up. I knew he was there, but I couldn't respond to him.

He ran to get Bobby, but he came back into the room with tears streaming down his face. He later told me that his father said, "If your mother is that stupid, then let her die." Instead, Darinn ran across the yard and pounded on my neighbor's door.

My friend and her husband rushed me to the emergency room. What I remember from that horrible night was my arms and ankles strapped to a hospital bed with tubes forced down my throat. I knew for sure I was going to die that night, but not from the pills I took. The nurses were going to be the ones to do it for me.

My next-door neighbor, Rowena, stayed by my side throughout the night, tightly holding my hand as water was pumped through one tube and my stomach contents flowed through the other. I tried to break free from the bands that held my wrists in place.

I gagged and arched my body, trying to stop the process, but no one stopped until they were finished. For a while, I was left alone. Tears stained my pillow. Was I crying because I still lived? Or did I feel shame from the darkest portion of my heart?

Later, a doctor came in the room asking me questions. He wanted to know if I had tried committing suicide before. I answered him, "No, this is my first time."

He said they were going to admit me, and I knew what that meant. They were going to lock me in a room and throw away the key. I grabbed hold of his arm and said that I would never do this again. My children needed me at home. Reality struck me, and I felt heart-wrenching guilt.

He patted me on my hand and said, "I understand." Then he walked away.

I tried to listen to whispered voices between the nurse and doctors, and then Rowena left her chair.

I kept saying, "I promise never to do this again, if you will just let me go home."

I had been there all night. I was exhausted and mentally drained, but I desperately wanted to go home. The doctor came back in and talked to me. I don't remember what he said, but I promised to seek professional help, and he allowed my friend to take me home.

When we drove into our driveway, Rowena helped me from the car and walked with me to my front door. The door was locked. She rang the doorbell quite a few times.

She looked at me strangely and said, "Where is your husband?" This was the first time Bobby's name was even mentioned.

Bobby finally came to the door, opening it just a crack. He took one look at me and slammed the door in my face. Rowena twisted the doorknob and it was open.

Rowena hugged me, and for a moment, I almost said, "Help me get away from here," but I didn't. I couldn't tell her—I was so ashamed of myself.

I called Belle within a few days. We had become friends, and I trusted her more than anyone else.

For days afterward, I would call her late into the night, and we talked for hours. I was still afraid to tell her that Bobby was physically abusive, but I sensed that she knew. Belle gave me the name of a therapist and made me promise to make an appointment.

Finally, I made an appointment with the therapist. I met with Jori several times before Bobby insisted on going with me.

Bobby complained about my emotional instability and how

difficult it was for him to live with me. He wanted Jori to cure me so we could repair our relationship.

Then Jori asked Bobby some personal questions, and he blew up at her. Flying from his chair, he leapt into her face and said she was a "bitch that hates men." Bobby exposed his true colors to Jori without me doing it for him, but Jori needed me to tell her and I couldn't do it.

During the week that followed, I became even more despondent. Waves and waves of anger thrashed inside me. I was angry with God. I was angry with Bobby, but most of all I hated the sight of myself.

I thought constantly about dying. It seemed to be the only answer for me. I was too angry to live and too wounded to leave. Dr. Stevens gave me all the help he could, but medication wasn't enough. Jori was there for me, but I was too afraid to open up to her.

Perhaps God really does works in mysterious ways. Even though I was silently wasting away, looking back I believe God's angels were busy at work. I had been praying for a miracle, and if miracles still happened, I was in desperate need of one.

Over the years, I had created my own Gethsemane, and I could no longer bear to carry the weight of my pain. My will to live had completely faded as surely as the flame on a candle fades in pouring rain, and once again I welcomed the thought of death.

In the still of the night, as I struggled with despair, the answer seemed so clear: it would be okay to end my life, since my children would be better off without a mother who had destroyed herself and failed to protect them against their violently abusive father.

I waited until everyone was asleep, and then I made my way into the kitchen and reached for the sleeping pills I had carefully stashed away. I knew exactly what needed to be done, and this time no one would find me.

With the pill bottle in my hand, I gently kissed my sleeping children good-bye.

Then I went into my bedroom and knelt by the bed. Somehow, I wanted to make peace with God before I took the pills. My heart was heavy as I prayed, *"Father in Heaven, why have you deserted me?"*

Tears covered my face, soaking my sheets and blanket.

"I need you, God. I don't want to live, but I just need to know why. Why would you abandon my children and me?"

I was so angry with God, yet in my most desperate hour I needed him more than ever before.

I begged him to answer me. *"Why, God, why have you done this to me?"*

I stayed on my knees for what seemed like forever, but I felt nothing. Foreboding silence claimed any hope I may have had.

My room was dark, cold, and empty—just as the life I lived was void of light. Shivering from the cold in the air, or perhaps from fear, I slowly climbed into bed, knowing God would never answer me.

I wrapped my arms tightly around myself, as if to say good-bye, and then I reached for the pills.

Suddenly, a glowing light appeared. Soft and subtle yet beautifully iridescent, it seemed to fill the space surrounding me with an answer I had been begging to hear.

A calm feeling came over me, silencing the sounds coming from my broken heart. Shimmering light flowed as a gentle stream into my body.

A tender love cradled me like a mother holding her newborn babe, and a voice I believed to be that of God gently whispered, *"My dear child, I am with you; I have always been with you."*

The radiant light that flooded my bedroom filled me with incredible strength. With sudden, inexplicable clarity, I felt separated, as though I was floating somewhere above my own body.

As I gazed down upon her face, her appearance was that of a heartbroken child.

In my heart I felt compassion for her, and even though it was my face I looked down upon, I seemed separate from and undamaged by her pain.

Then, just as quickly as I felt myself above my body, I returned.

I felt the presence of angel wings fluttering above my pillow as tiny threads of fine light seemed to flow throughout my body. The power of this light was dramatically healing my emotional body. As if in fast motion, I felt healing taking place—the same as you would physically if you had an open flesh wound. Then all during the night, incredible love comforted me.

I felt courage, hope, and a sense of power swell into the birthing of new life.

Surrounded by love, I felt an infusion of knowledge that I hadn't understood before.

For many years, I had been mistaken. God had never abandoned me; it was I who had forsaken God.

Sleep did not come for many hours, and long into the first rays of early morning light, a soft whispering voice let me know that soon my mission would unfold. For the time being, I was to leave my husband.

Many things I had yet to understand, but I was also promised that I would have the guidance I needed and many doors would open for me with opportunities to live the life I was meant to live.

Without a doubt, I believe God and His angels intervened. Without this divine intervention, I don't know that I would have ever found the courage and the strength to get away from my abusive husband.

Years of violence, the police at my door, fraud charges, and Bobby's true exposure were finally enough to give me permission to break the vows of silence. Our "Biblical Marriage "was not sacred or sealed forever. It was a sin against God and our Eternal Mother for me to stay and be harmed. And the power was mine to do what should have been done fifteen years ago.

In the past, I had stayed away from family as much as I could, but I now realized they couldn't help as long as I wouldn't let them know how. Later that afternoon, I called my sister Marsha and told her I was leaving my husband. She said, "Oh, Janice, it's about time."

When I finally confided in my sister, it felt as though the weight of the world was lifted. I begged her not to tell my mother, and she promised she wouldn't.

Ten minutes after I hung up the phone, I received a call from my mother, and she said, "Marsha just called me, how can I help?"

From that minute on, my mother became my strength.

"We'll get through this together," she promised.

My mother offered to help me move into another home. Since I didn't have a car, she told me to look for a used car, and she would send me the money to pay for it.

I convinced my husband I needed time to be alone to get well. Since we were losing yet another home in foreclosure, it was mutually agreed that he would stay where we were until the foreclosure sale.

I allowed him to believe he would move in with the children and me when that was finished.

During the week, my husband helped me move furniture into the home I had rented, believing he would soon follow. Once I actually set my plan into motion, there was no turning back. I knew my life depended upon it.

I had to get away from him if I were to survive.

11

Leaving Put My Life at Risk

Sometime in your life you will go on a journey. It will be the longest journey you have ever taken. It is the journey to find yourself.
—*Kathleen Sharp*

I was scared, or perhaps in a state of shock realizing I had finally taken that terrifying first step—the one I had been unable to make for so many years. At first, life seemed surreal.

I had lived in fear all those years, but finally, in 1992, nothing else mattered. I wasn't responsible for taking care of Bobby. I couldn't do it anymore; I had to take care of me. Finally I was angry enough that I didn't feel anything else. I wasn't feeling the same fear I did before, the helplessness, or even guilt enough to feel sorry for him. I was so angry from all that he had done to my children and to me; going so far as to use my severe depression as a way to humiliate me and threaten to use it against me if I tried to leave him only fueled my rage.

I also knew that if I stayed one more day he would break my spirit. Slipping into that dark underworld was real to me. Little by little, bits and pieces of me washed away. Every insult and humiliation left unhealed wounds because I wasn't even allowed to *feel* them. Unlike the fictional story of Alice following the rabbit into the burrow and finding a merry, topsy-turvy world of Wonderland, mine was an angry world with six very young and traumatized children.

Many times, the only place I felt safe enough to cry was in my bathroom. I still remember sitting in the tub with the water running and sobbing, I didn't want my children to see me so distraught when they needed me most, yet I couldn't hide it from them either.

I may have been getting up each day, but my heart had shriveled into this dried pitiful prune pit. I was consumed with anger and frightened that I couldn't feel anything else. I don't know if this was a reason, but I also did many things of which I am ashamed.

I can remember walking into a store, stuffing merchandise into my purse, and brazenly walking out of the store as if it didn't matter. I hated what I was doing, but at least I felt in control. Stealing released a sudden rush of adrenaline. I felt alive and in control. Admitting this sounds like a poor excuse for intolerable behavior, but I was in a poor state of thinking.

One morning, I took a long hard look into my bathroom mirror. The face of the woman staring back at me frightened me so much that reality finally started to sink in. I couldn't believe the reflection was me, but the freedom I felt as I saw my own reflection gave me the courage to gently touch my face and feel the emptiness in my heart. I wept that morning, knowing how much of me the abuse had destroyed.

I really *was* sick. Emotionally, I had been destroyed. My mother did the best she could under the circumstances, but I don't think anyone realized the severity of my depression. I wasn't capable of taking care of six children without help. They needed stability in their life, and I couldn't offer that to them emotionally. I know I further traumatized them by my own behavior. What they saw in me was frightening. One moment I would be okay, the next they would find me huddled in a corner sobbing because I couldn't face cleaning the kitchen or fixing them breakfast.

Perhaps entering a shelter would have been more appropriate for the kids and me at that time, but I didn't do it. Instead, I found a way to leave Bobby without facing the reality that I couldn't take care of my children or myself, and that my life was still in danger.

Soon Bobby began to pressure me. It was time for him to be together with his family, he said. I wasn't emotionally competent to live on my own. I needed him to help me recover from depression and control the older boys' behavior. One afternoon, he began moving his personal belongings into my bedroom, and I knew it was time to tell him he wasn't welcome.

I was as prepared as I could be when I told him I was filing for divorce, and I wanted him to stay away from the children and me. First he didn't believe me, and then he went ballistic. He grabbed me, and I struggled until I got away. With only the bed between us, he screamed, "You will find yourself in hell if you ever try leaving me."

Frightened, I tried to grab the phone, but he ripped it out of the wall. We screamed at each other. I yelled at him to leave, and he shouted that I still belonged to him, and I had ruined his life so I had to stay and pay for the years he put up living with me.

Before I knew it, Bobby had a hold of me, throwing me onto my bed with his hands around my neck. But this was a woman he had never reckoned with before, because this time I fought back.

A raging force built inside of me, and with all my might I drew my knees into my abdomen, and then with a powerful force I kicked him.

He was startled as he fell backward. Scrambling to my feet, I grabbed a clothes hamper (it was the only thing close enough to me) and began swinging it.

Before he had a chance to react, I was wildly screaming and

beating him with unbelievable strength. Over and over I beat him with the empty clothes hamper—he didn't have a chance to hit me back.

Years of imprisoned rage wanted to see him dead as I screamed, "It is your turn to live in hell. If you ever touch me again, I will have you thrown in jail!"

I don't know that I was physically hurting him, but I was wild with fury, screaming uncontrollably that I would kill him. Completely thrown off guard, Bobby backed away from me. Once he did, I threw down my only weapon and told him the house was in my name, the car was in my name, and I would file for a restraining order against him if I had to.

Triumphant that I had finally stood up to him, I yelled in his face, "Get the hell out of my house."

He grabbed some of his personal belongings and turned around to leave, but not before saying, "I'll be back, I promise you that."

For the first time, I didn't feel sorry for him. I didn't feel guilty for hurting him or taking anything away from him like I had in the past. Many times in the past, I didn't call the police because I didn't want my children to see their father handcuffed and taken off to jail. I also didn't want to see him suffer, even though it was okay for me to suffer for him. Thinking about how *he* felt had been my life story, but today I was thinking about me.

For weeks, he watched every move I made. I could see him following me, and I saw him drive slowly by my house every evening to make sure I was still there. He would telephone me late into the night and beg me to forgive him. He even said he would go to counseling.

I told him he was about fifteen years too late. I would never take him back. Then he threatened to kill himself, but I didn't care.

I told him he deserved to die for what he had done to me and his own children. I told him hell was too good for him.

Unable to control my anger, I wanted him to hurt as much as he had hurt me. He may have been remorseful for a few minutes, but as soon as I said, "People like you don't deserve to live, and I promise you this, I will *never* come back to you," Bobby was no longer repentant. Instead, he was just as vile and dangerous as before.

He said. "I'll ruin your life if you destroy mine by leaving me."

I knew Bobby meant every word. He swore he would take away the kids, and I would never see them again. He promised to shout to the whole world each and every one of my dark secrets, and I knew exactly what he meant by that.

"Everyone," he said, "will know the whole truth about you." The war was on. Bobby wasn't going to let me walk away without a fight, and I was frantic.

Friends in my ward listened to Bobby's side of the story. Rumors spread. Stories of my attempted suicide reached every ear willing to listen. Many sided with my estranged husband, feeling sorry for him that I wrecked his life by spending all his money and then leaving him destitute and taking his children away from him.

How could people listen to his lies? Why were they so quick to judge me? An older man who had known me since birth had recently moved into our ward. His comment was, "I never see Janice at church and yet her husband attends faithfully, so just who are we to believe?"

To make matters worse, the bishop in my new ward didn't want to help me. He was more concerned about contributing to the breakup of a family than he was about protecting victims of violence. And besides, according to him, what proof did he have that my husband beat me?

Infuriated, my dear friend Belle told him, "Do you want to be responsible for this woman's death?" After Belle made that comment, he agreed to help.

Finally, I made an appointment with a divorce attorney. He

was aggressive, and he also knew Bobby. He was ready to fight fire with fire.

But I was afraid to cross Bobby. I didn't want Bobby served with divorce papers, and so I thought I could work with him amicably once he knew I was not going to reconcile.

One night, I awakened from a sound sleep around three a.m. to find Bobby sitting on the floor next to my bed.

I had no idea how long he had been sitting there, but as I was waking up he kept mumbling that he had put up with me for all these years and would never let me leave.

Panicked, I didn't know what to do. My phone was by the bed, but if I made the wrong move I knew Bobby would react violently. So I pretended to still be asleep.

Bobby was rocking back and forth, telling me how much he loved me and that his life was not worth living without me.

My heart was pounding, and I was afraid he would try to get into bed with me. Silently, I prayed, begging God to protect me. *Please just make him go.*

Then Bobby started chanting, "You will have to die," over and over. Then he stopped rocking and stood up.

Leaning down into my face, he whispered, "I'll never let anyone else have you, because you belong to me." My heart nearly stopped. I wasn't breathing, but I could hardly keep from screaming.

I could feel Bobby's heavy breathing, and I knew he was staring at me, but I kept my eyes tightly closed. Then Bobby turned around and walked out of my room.

Relief swept through me, and I started sobbing. I felt God had somehow protected me, but I wasn't going to give Bobby another chance to test my faith in God or in the legal system.

The next morning, I made new plans.

I called a friend, asking her if she would be interested in buying my furniture. Margie bought and sold used furniture as a business.

I explained that I was divorcing Bobby, and I needed to get out of town as soon as possible.

Later that day, Margie came over and agreed to buy most of what I had. She left me a check along with an invoice listing each piece of furniture she had purchased. Margie knew she was to pick up the furniture after I vacated the house without letting Bobby know anything about it.

That afternoon, I made the mistake of leaving the invoice on the kitchen table. Bobby walked into my house, uninvited, and made his way into the kitchen before I knew he was there. Running down the stairs, I demanded that he leave immediately. He must have a suspicious nose letting him know when I was up to something, because he was certainly suspicious that afternoon.

"What are you trying to hide from me?" he demanded to know.

I wouldn't answer him, except to tell him he had no right to there and I wanted him out. Then he saw the invoice. He grabbed it from the kitchen table and read it. Detailed on the invoice was every piece of furniture I sold, including items he had made. I panicked and started moving toward the sliding-glass door.

He jumped in front of me, waving the invoice in my face. He first grabbed me by the arm while dragging me through the house, forcing me to show him exactly what I had sold, reminding me that the table, the armoire, and the hutch were items he owned. Nothing, he said, was mine.

Twisting my arm, he demanded I give him the money she had given me. Lying through my teeth, I swore Margie hadn't paid me yet.

Bobby shoved me against the wall. He was angry because I wouldn't let him move in, and this was the proof he needed to show my intent to leave him. The first blow I felt was in my stomach as I doubled over. He threw another punch, knocking me to the floor.

Each time Bobby kicked me with his boot, he called me filthy names.

Screaming for help, I tried to protect myself. Robby heard me and came running. Once he saw his dad, he yelled at him to stop. Robby tried getting in between Bobby and me, but Bobby threw him against the wall.

Robby ran from the room, and seconds later he returned, furiously trying to stop Bobby as he frantically screamed, "I've called the police, leave my mom alone." Bobby kicked me again, swearing he wasn't through with me. He ran, slammed the door, and raced off in his pickup.

Rob was bluffing, and for a moment I was amazed and shocked at what just happened. Perhaps when I took the first step to own my power, my son had the courage to act on his.

For the first time, I wasn't submitting to Bobby's threats, and he was losing the ultimate weapon he had over me because I was no longer feeling sorry for him. He was losing, and that was something he would never let happen. Not only had I refused to let him move in with me, threatening to divorce him, but I had sold his furniture. Bobby had once beaten his boys senseless because they broke a jar containing old marbles that belonged to him. What I did was worse. If I didn't give the money to Bobby, my very life was in danger, and I knew Bobby would soon return again.

He called me later that afternoon just to remind me that he would be there the following day to pick up his money, and I damn sure better have it for him. I reassured him that I would.

Bobby had started delivering newspapers in the afternoon just before I left him, and before he had to be at work he would drive by my house checking up on me. Then, as soon as he was through delivering papers, he would drive by my house again before going home. But on weekends, he had to start his delivery route just before midnight.

I knew Bobby would be gone for two or three hours, and that would give me enough time. I arranged with friends from my church to arrive at my house just after Bobby left for his paper route to help me pack my things into a U-Haul trailer.

I waited until I saw Bobby drive by my house, and then I made the phone call. The men were waiting at Belle's house, not too far from where I lived. I was frantic. I was so afraid something would go awry, and Bobby would drive up before we were finished.

Everyone was madly dashing around the house grabbing whatever they could and throwing it inside the van. As soon as we had packed all we could, the men left and I ran to get the kids, who were sleeping on the floor in an empty bedroom. I needed to get them into my Suburban before it was too late.

Afraid to say anything to my kids, I didn't tell them my plans. Rob and Darinn woke up when the men arrived at the house, and they helped with the packing, but my four younger ones cried as soon as I told them we had to hurry and leave. Once it dawned on them what we were doing, they didn't want to go.

Each minute that was wasted was precious time. I didn't have time to be gentle or reassuring, and they resisted getting their clothes on, complaining that they didn't want to leave their friends. They didn't want to leave their bikes and toys that we didn't have room to take. My five-year-old wanted to say good-bye to his dad; my three-year-old just wanted to go back to sleep.

I wanted to yell at all of them, "Just shut up and get in the damn car," but I didn't because we were all extremely stressed. I just wanted to get out of there.

Finally, I had my kids settled in. They had blankets and pillows, and I strapped them in best I could. Then I had to open the garage door. Shadows seemed to lurk behind the bushes, and I was shaking as I cautiously opened the garage door. A soft wind rustled dried leaves, causing my heart to skip a beat. I expected Bobby to jump out of the dark at any moment.

Nighttime always intensified my fear, and if Bobby caught me he would beat the life out of me. But I didn't see anyone on the streets.

The night air was deadly still. Hurriedly, I jumped into the car and turned on the ignition. My heart was pounding as I pulled out of the driveway and began to drive away from the house. I glanced at the time, and it was 1:30 in the morning. Bobby would be on his way home. I didn't know which street he would be taking, but I was terrified that he would see me by the time I reached Country Club Drive.

Quivering, I wasn't thinking straight. Once I made it out of the subdivision, I headed in the wrong direction, and I didn't dare go back out of fear that Bobby would be looking for me. I parked my car in back of a grocery store and waited for nearly an hour, but the longer I waited the closer I felt to having a heart attack.

A friend was driving the U-Haul to a town close to the border, but she wasn't going to leave for several more hours. Finally, I decided to get out of Mesa as fast as I could. Once back out on the street, I prayed, and I drove as fast as I dared. We made it to the freeway with no sight of Bobby. Relieved, I felt the worse was over.

As I crossed the Arizona border into Mexico, I felt freedom— like a caged bird realizing she had broken wings but her strength of will would carry her through the night. I looked back at the life I lived and the life I nearly ended and vowed to be free.

I was going to get well.

After we arrived in Mexico, my children and I stayed with my mother, but I knew our stay could only be temporary. We needed a place of our own. There were seven of us, and we were adding stress to my mother's life, and that put more stress on me. One afternoon, my mom and I went for a drive.

I wasn't sure I was going to stay in Mexico, but when we passed a vacant house, I told her to stop and we got out. We both walked through weeds up to our waist and peeked in through the windows.

The house had been vacant for quite some time, and it was rather small for a family of seven, but I was excited.

"Mom, this is it," I said. "This is where I need to live until my divorce is final."

With my mother's help, we talked to the owners and an agreement was reached. This little red brick house, facing Main Street, built over a hundred years ago, was soon to be my first real home—far enough away from any threat of violence.

The weather was humid and hot, but I had help cleaning the house. What I loved about the house was the wood flooring after we stripped off the worn vinyl. Then I found the most amazing piece of antique furniture stored in the cellar. It was an original cupboard taken out of the kitchen. Of course, we carried it back up the stairway, clearing away the spiderwebs, and out into the open so I could polish it up. Then every window was opened in the house to let the warm summer breeze in, which was also the only air-conditioning we had.

I saw new life all around me. Even though our small two-bedroom house appeared shabby in the beginning, it was more than safe. This old creaky house that really had its issues was our sanctuary, and in spite of the problems we still faced, at least we had a chance to heal.

Outside in the flower beds, tiny buds seemed to whisper sweet promises of new beginnings. For the first time, I felt that I had a life and I could do anything I wanted with it. I wasn't weeping at the drop of a hat; instead, I was finally starting to breath without feeling suffocated or anxiously worrying about doing something wrong.

Summer was soon over, and the children began a new school year. They seemed to be thriving in a new environment without living under tremendous stress. They were playing as normal children and bringing friends into our home, where they knew they would be respected and treated with dignity.

Once Bobby was served with divorce papers, I believe he knew our marriage was over and that I wasn't returning, but he wasn't ready to give up. He fought the divorce and filed a petition with the court seeking sole custody on the grounds that I was an unfit parent and alleging I left the country taking the children without his permission.

I fought against his petition, but in a court hearing I was unable to introduce allegations of spousal and child abuse because none had been reported. Instead, he was allowed to introduce hospital records and suicidal letters from me to my children, and the judge ruled against me.

Temporarily, I lost my battle to keep my children in Mexico. I was ordered to return to Arizona, even though we had no place to live and I was unemployed. The fact that Bobby was not paying child support was a separate issue, but I left the courtroom vowing I would never allow Bobby to manipulate his way through the court system. He didn't want full custody of six children. He wanted to punish me and force me back to him.

12

Revealing the Pain

Learn to get in touch with the silence within yourself
and know that everything in this life has a purpose.
—Elisabeth Kübler-Ross

L ife is not a fairy tale, and frogs don't turn into princes when you
kiss them. Instead, when you're married to an abuser, you turn
into the frog. My own self-reflection, the worn-out woman revealed
years of stress and pain.

Just as I was trying to make a better life for my children—
without any child support from him—Bobby was doing everything
he could to uproot them. He represented himself in court; I had to
hire an attorney. I was so afraid of losing my children. Bobby was
right, I did leave the country, and I certainly didn't do it with his
permission.

For months, I traveled back and forth from Mexico to Mesa
so I could continue my therapy with Jori as well as appear in court
when I had to.

In the beginning, I wanted Bobby to acknowledge what he had
done, as if that would make everything all better. But Bobby wasn't

going to show up at Jori's willing to beg my forgiveness and tell me how sorry he felt for what he had done.

Broken bones and bruises long since vanished were no longer visible but the emotional wounds were deep. Psychological abuse from verbal and emotional battering daily had caused damage in my life and that of my children. So instead of expecting Bobby to man up, I did the next best thing.

I used imagery. I visualized scenes in which I was being beaten. This time, I couldn't allow myself to shut down. I had already done that; it's a natural human instinct to protect the mechanism that keeps us functioning, which is our mind. First, I told him why we were in therapy and how angry I was at him for hurting me.

It was difficult to relive moments of sheer terror, but I was safe in Jori's office, and that provided the security I needed.

When I lived with Bobby, I was always conscious of whether or not I felt safe in a room. I would stay close to any door that offered a quick escape, and I was always frightened of going into the bathroom or closet where he could corner me. So in my mind, I pictured an open door, an easy escape if he lost his temper, and then I mustered up my most vivid imagination, which isn't all that bad, and I recreated actual memories of violence.

The terror I felt remembering the rage in his eyes and his strength was enough for me to say, "I'm not going there." But I had to relive it—somehow it had to become real enough for me to feel the terror and how I felt and associate with it in order for me to deal with it.

My most vivid recollection was the time he used the golf club. I can't even begin to describe it in detail. It was excruciating, but what frightened me more than anything was the thought of my unborn baby.

As I described the scene to Jori, I closed my eyes. I remembered watching him as he ran to the golf bag standing in the corner and, in haste, grabbed a golf club. Everything happened in split seconds.

There wasn't enough time to run, but I knew exactly what he was going to do with that awful thing.

Then I watched, as if in slow motion, as he swung the club into the air and brought it crashing down on me. That's when the pain hit me also. I actually felt it rip into my skin. I wanted to stop, but I didn't.

I let my mind carry me all the way through it, each painful swing, one after another. I remembered crawling on my hands and knees, trying to escape the next blow.

I was scared, not only for my life, but also for my baby's life, and I relived each terrorizing moment until the beating stopped.

When necessary, I would reenact another situation in which I felt helpless; I had fifteen years' worth of accumulated memories, so it wasn't that difficult. I brought it to life the best way I could, and instead of cowering, I stood up to him.

In my make-believe game, I was the one who could do anything I wanted. I needed to play it over and over just long enough to say, *"No one will ever do this to me again."*

Then I took all the humiliation I felt over the years and handed it back to him. "This is yours," I said. "I no longer need to feel it. It's your turn to feel what you did to me."

In time, I found I didn't really need to hurt him; I just needed to stop him from hurting me. I didn't feel better by causing him to huddle defensively in a corner—I didn't want to be that horrible giant hurting someone else. But it felt good to stand up to him and take away the power he had over me, and it was a necessary step in my recovery.

Each time I replayed this scene, truth would hit me in the face. Bobby was an abuser when I married him—he always had been, and he never changed. I was the one trying to change him. I wanted so badly for him to see the dysfunction in his behavior that I forgot to look at mine. What seemed astonishing to me was that he never once saw any need to change his behavior; he was too busy trying to change me.

Jori helped me understand that battered women disassociate with their own real feelings, and they begin identifying with how the abuser feels. Once I felt safe enough to talk about the abuse, the dam broke, because I also gave myself permission to *feel* my pain. I mattered. My feelings mattered, and stuffing them made me ill and distorted the way I felt about myself.

Knowing that I didn't have to take any of his cruelty anymore and that I was willing and able to stand up for my self was the most liberating feeling of all. In triumph, I felt renewed, with a power I hadn't experienced before.

Most of all, I had to accept that I enabled—I was codependent. With that awareness, I took responsibility for my recovery. Blaming him or anyone else only victimized me more, but seeing the role I played helped me take a deep look at myself. I had taken many blows to not only to my physical body but also to my self-esteem.

I also needed to understand why I allowed others to control my decisions, why I went to my clergy for guidance and for sustainment over and over again. While this may be common for battered women, women of my faith are also taught the sanctity of marriage and to honor their marriage vows. Others are ingrained with the doctrine of subjugation and are easily controlled and manipulated. It's also an embarrassment to let anyone know that you are in an abusive relationship.

In view of all that had gone before, it really was difficult for me to understand why my bishops hadn't understood what was happening inside my family enough to do something about it when I asked for help.

They knew of the abuse, so why didn't I receive their support to leave my husband?

What difference did it make if Bobby attended his meetings? It didn't change him.

What difference did it make if I attended the temple with my husband? Attending the temple didn't cure either one of us because it isn't possible to find healing inside an abusive relationship.

It is important for me to listen to my own instincts. To feel what is in my own sacred heart. If I'm unwilling or unable to access this feminine power, then something is wrong. Something is out of alignment within my inner system—my inner self.

I am deserving of my sovereignty, which according to my own upbringing, according to God, is my absolute right to do all things according to my own conscience. But to know what is right for me—not according to someone else's opinion—I have to know how I feel, who I really am, and what I really want.

Without even knowing where to start, I just knew I was starting over. A breakdown really is a breakthrough, a time of discarding (dumping) all my usual patterns to allow a transformation to take shape, kind of a metamorphosis that necessitates the destruction of the old that holds back new development.

How often are we willing to give up our differences, our own uniqueness, for approval? If we act or feel like others want us to in order to receive their approval, what we lose is our own identity. We also lose much more as they gain more control over our lives. But if we seek true joy and connection with life, we must heal these unfulfilled needs and dissolve our masks to express our true and deep authenticity.

In facing my past, I faced a lot of ugliness. My behavior had been humiliating. Instead of hating myself, I needed to put my arms around myself, comfort the little girl in me, and begin to learn how to love her. This became my first and most important step to recovery. My past was an accumulation of many experiences, and by allowing all that hurt into my life, I was wounded. So were my children. But none of what I experienced defined who I really am.

Yet there was a fracture, a break between my soul and my human side or personality—the subconscious aspect where everything of the unhealed past is stored. Some call it the "shadow self." Others call it the "walking wounded"or"pained bodies." Unfortunately, we can't just walk away from that pain; we must walk through it. We have to face it, own it, and feel it before we can heal and release it.

13

Children Caught in the Middle

Each day it was my prayer to find my saving grace—
what did I need to make it through each day?
Sometimes I just needed help with my children.

While the judge was deciding Bobby's petition for custody, I was ordered to bring the kids across the border and meet him somewhere in between on specified weekends so he could pick them up. I didn't want to, and I made up excuses when I could, but I had to comply with the judge's ruling.

During this time, there was just chaos. Despite feelings of helplessness with the judicial system and an infuriation with Bobby, there wasn't anything I could do to hold him responsible for the irrational things he would do. Bobby would always do or say something to hurt the kids just to get back at me.

One time they were to stay with their dad for two weeks during Easter vacation. A few days after they arrived, Bobby became angry over something that happened and told the kids to get out of his apartment. Robby called me collect from a pay phone telling me that he and the other kids had been told to leave, and they were forced to sit outside in the parking lot. It took me seven hours to get there, and during that time they waited in the sweltering hot Arizona sun.

I can't begin to imagine the rejection they must have felt. Remembering those awful years is difficult. My children endured so much.

Robby and I continued to struggle in our relationship. Terribly defiant, he didn't want to get up in the morning. He refused to attend church, and he was disrespectful. He got angry when I tried forcing him to do anything, and then he accused me of being a liar.

Robby told me that he could never respect me as his mother. Taken aback by the hostility in his voice, I asked him why.

"How could you have an abortion, Mom? God will never forgive you because of the things you did."

I was stunned. I asked Rob who told him, and he answered, "Dad told me, and he said you would only deny it if I asked you." Apparently, Bobby wanted his son to know exactly what kind of mother he had.

Shocked beyond words that Bobby would do this to his own son, I tried to explain to Robby what had happened, but he didn't want to listen. In anguish, I wanted to wither and die. I was humiliated in front of my son trying to defend my actions and explain why I had opted to have an abortion, but he was only thirteen years old.

My children were also trying to see through the lies and deception and work through the hurt and betrayal. In order to love their dad, did they have to hate their mother? They were also angry with their dad because they had been so mistreated, verbally and physically, but he was part of them. By hating him, my son said one day, isn't that the same as hating myself?

I was learning how difficult it was to parent with the same unhealthy codependent behavior I had as a wife. *Codependency* is a word used to describe unhealthy behavior between two people. In my marriage, it could have meant that the marriage (or relationship) meant more to me than I meant to myself. It could also mean that I didn't feel deserving of anyone better; therefore, I had to put up with his abuse. But I also feel that as a child, if we seek love through pain, as an adult we will accept pain as a way to be loved.

There are many good self-help books written on this subject. One I recommend highly is Melody Beattie's *Codependent No More*. From experience, I will never forget how difficult it was to parent at the same time I was in recovery—not recovered—from the abuse or healed from severe depression, and my children had yet to even begin.

No one had any boundaries. My children certainly didn't. They were going to do whatever they wanted when they wanted. Since I was the adult, it was up to me to teach and enforce and encourage my children in a loving environment, but this is where it gets a little tough. Three of them were hardly children, and the next two really became followers.

We've learned to take the bad and cherish the good. I feel it was the laughing in the beginning and the sharing of our deepest feelings that started our family healing. We started spending time talking and doing things together.

Even though some incidents are rather insignificant, I remember one afternoon when Darinn, age eleven, and Westin, age three, were playing a game they called "Cowboy." Darinn would throw a looped rope around Westin's head and pretend he was roping a calf.

One afternoon, Darinn got the rope out and said, "Come on, Wes, let's play."

Westin put his little hands on his hips and said, "Okay, but I'm tired of playing that way. This time I'll be the boy and you can be the cow."

We laughed until we cried, and for the first time, I realized that we could say or do anything without being afraid.

Unfortunately for all of us but especially my children, I really struggled with depression and taking care of six children who had their share of problems. When I couldn't cope, I took more pills. Sometimes you really just have to put it out there, no matter how many years have passed or how many times you say, "I can't believe I'm not beyond that." Today it still hurts that I emotionally hurt my children.

The only antidepressant that seemed to help was Prozac, but that wasn't enough. I already had prescriptions for Ambien and Xanax from my doctor in Arizona, and our family doctor in Mexico prescribed Ativan for me. Even then, I was abusing the medication. I was depending on prescription drugs to get me through each day.

Before long, I was also plagued by chronic fatigue. I don't know what brought it on so suddenly, but most of the time it was incapacitating.

The judge finally ordered a family evaluation, so I had to prepare my children. This made them even more confused. What were they supposed to say against their father? In fact, they didn't want to talk about the abuse with anyone, they just wanted their lives to be normal, and they wanted their father to treat them with kindness.

Even though my children hated their father's abuse, they still loved him, and they needed to know he loved them. When we, as parents, are angry and feel the need to get even, we should remember how devastating it is for our children to hear insulting remarks about either of their parents—however true they may be—because both parents will always be a part of their identity.

Much later, my son Robby allowed me to read part of his diary. He wrote: "My mother is having a hard time, I feel bad for her. I wish we could stay here but my dad is trying to make us go back. I like my new home if only my mother wasn't so sad."

Nine months later, in 1993, my divorce was final, although the child-custody issue had not been settled. The day I received the news from my attorney, I celebrated. Yet, to be truthful, there wasn't much *to* celebrate—too much damage had been done, and I had to wonder if we would ever heal.

We had been living in Mexico for nearly sixteen months when I returned to Arizona with my children for psychological testing, and I found the process to be very complicated.

After a few days of evaluation, I cancelled the visits and refused to have my children continue with the process because Bobby refused to attend. He was the one the judge had ordered to pay for the children's evaluations. The psychiatrist was blackmailing me into paying instead. The afternoon of our second day, the psychiatrist took me in his office, closing the door behind him.

"As you can see, your ex-husband cancelled every appointment we have made with him, but someone has to pay for your children and obviously, he isn't here today to do it."

Shocked by what he said, I answered him, "Take that up with him, I'm doing my part. I've paid you for my evaluation"—just as the judge ordered—"now Bobby is responsible for theirs."

I got up to leave, but he insisted I hear him out. What he wanted me to understand was that it was up to him to decide our fate. "If you don't come up with the money by tomorrow morning, I'll write an unsatisfactory report against you."

Infuriated, I stood up and told him, "Do what you have to do, but you won't receive one more dime from me." I hardly had the money to pay for mine, and since I refused to pay for evaluations the judge ordered my ex-husband to pay for, he did write an unsatisfactory report against me.

Life can be anything but fair, but the judge didn't control every aspect of my life, and thank heaven angels were still busy at work. Even though I struggled with my children, I wasn't discouraged.

During the next few months, intuitively, I felt excitement in the air. Something was going to change, and I felt it would be good for both my life and that of my children.

14

Someone to Love and Stand Beside Me

To be touched by love is to open our hearts to our own vulnerability.
Only then can we begin to grow and experience life in splendid
color, and find a true friendship that will last forever.

Precognitive dreams—vivid dreams that feel so real they are strongly with you once you wake—became part of my life. Some dreams came in the form of a warning of what would happen should I not change my behavior. Often I would dream of things that were to happen, and later they did. In the beginning, I resented these dreams. They frightened me. Later I saw them as a gift and another way spirit communicates with us.

In the meantime, I felt magic in the air. The countryside was aglow in vivid autumn colors. Early morning walks gave me time alone to experience the wonder of this special feeling. My children were busy in school and looking forward to the upcoming Christmas holidays.

They hadn't seen their father for several months, and the court date for the custody hearing had been changed until sometime in January 1996. Bobby and I hadn't called a truce, but the kids needed to find a place of neutrality.

After Bobby's divorce from his deceased twin brother's wife, he began dating someone else he met from his apartment complex, and it wasn't long before they were married. Bobby hadn't been paying child support, and when I learned he was given a temple recommend, I called his current bishop.

The man's response was ice-cold. I was accused of causing severe suffering in the life of my ex-husband. It was his opinion that Bobby had done nothing to deserve the abandonment of his family or my harassment for child support, since Bobby could barely maintain his own needs. This was another rude awakening for me.

It was late November when my mother told me about her plans to be with my sisters in Salt Lake City, Utah. She tried to encourage me to go with her, but I felt certain I would have other plans. Call it woman's intuition, but I had no doubt that I wouldn't be alone on Christmas Eve. A few days later, a friend of mine told me of his cousin who was divorced and living in Tucson, Arizona.

Don called Richard. He waited until the following day, and in their conversation, Jay told Richard about me. In fact, according to Don, he made me sound exciting enough that having six children at home seemed (almost) insignificant.

Richard was to call me the following Sunday. Anxiously, I waited for that day. I counted the hours. I was excited and extremely curious, and finally it was Sunday. I made sure my kids were busy watching television.

All of them cooperated, but Justin was suspicious. He wanted to know why I didn't want him in the same room with the telephone and me.

Finally, I told him that I was waiting for a guy to call me. That was a big mistake.

The minute the phone rang, I knew it was Richard, but Justin grabbed the phone before I could. Reluctantly, he passed the phone to me, but then he started to argue.

I didn't want Richard to hear the commotion, so I begged Justin to wait until I was through talking. I had tried explaining to Justin that this was just a friendly conversation and that he shouldn't feel threatened.

Finally, I asked Richard to hold on. I ran for Rob. Rob was strong enough to drag Justin out of the room and keep him away from me, and Rob was only too happy to oblige.

I ran with the phone, closing myself off in the bathroom while Rob and Justin fought with one another. Rob grabbed Justin by the legs and pulled him outside and then sat on him. Unfortunately, I could still hear Justin screaming.

Richard and I stayed on the phone for nearly an hour. There I was, huddled in the bathroom, sitting on the toilet seat with the water running and the door closed so he couldn't hear Justin. Richard's voice was soothing, loving, kind, and gentle, and he had a wonderful sense of humor.

I melted into a puddle of emotions sitting on that toilet lid. I had no idea what Richard looked like, but that didn't have any bearing on my feelings.

We made plans that afternoon. I was to take my children to Mesa on December 21 to drop them off at their dad's home, and then I would spend the night at a friend's and return to Tucson by noon the following day. That day soon arrived.

Just off the freeway, as you first enter Tucson's city limits, is a McDonalds. Richard said to stop there and call him. He lived just minutes away, and once I called he would meet me there.

Nervously, I pulled into the parking lot. The telephone was inside the restaurant near the restrooms. Timidly, I walked in, knowing I had to call him, but I was so nervous. I went into the bathroom, stared at the face in the mirror, and couldn't help but wonder, *"Am I still pretty enough?"*

I left the bathroom and stood by the pay phone. Hours could

have passed or just minutes, but I know I stood there for a long time and still I didn't dare dial his number. That's when a stranger walked up to me, and looking right at me, he started to speak.

For a moment, my heart stopped. *"If this is him,"* I thought to myself, *"I'm running."* I wasn't the least bit interested in the looks of this man.

With a blank look on my face, I didn't let him say a word before I asked him if he was waiting to meet someone, and he said, "No, but I would like to use the phone, so if you're not going to call anyone, would you please move out of the way?"

Relief washed over me as I nervously laughed and said, "Thank God you're not Richard." That's when I found the courage to call him; he couldn't look any worse than that stranger.

I told him what I was wearing, and that I would be waiting outside the front door of McDonald's. I thought I would die a thousand deaths before he got there, and then all of a sudden there he was. He recognized me instantly. He knew my mother and said I looked just like her.

I was still so nervous, I hardly said a word, but I remember following behind him in my car. Over a dusty unpaved road, I sped to keep up with him.

I thought about many things in a short period of time. Life had given me many hard lessons, and I was still trying to grasp the strangeness of this whole situation. Richard's face wasn't familiar at all, yet my feelings were overwhelming. For a split second, I wanted to turn my car around and drive across the desert and disappear into the fading sunset.

Then I thought, *"No, I'll stop and sit in the hot, scorching sun until reason returns."* That shouldn't take long; even in December, the desert is hot in mid-afternoon. I was willing to ask anyone who would listen, even if my only audience was prairie dogs, if they thought I was a fool for allowing my heart to feel again, to love and to trust again.

129

I didn't turn around. Instead, I followed him to his front door, and once inside, I felt at home. It was as though I had been there before. We talked for hours, not as strangers, but as one in heart and spirit. When I looked into his eyes, the windows to his soul, I knew I had no secrets from him. He knew me, he really knew me.

Years of pain dimmed. A heart once betrayed felt renewed, alive, and so filled with joy. I felt myself wanting to reach out and hold on to him, love him, or curse him for making me go through life without him. *"Where have you been?"* My heart seemed to say.

Richard wanted to know everything about me, including my past. I was open and honest with him from the very beginning, and he knew that my family had been through a lot from domestic violence. I was recovering, but I still had a long way to go. For years, I had battled against debilitating depression, and it wasn't that long ago.

I couldn't tell him enough. It was the sharing I longed for; just conversing with him was healing. He felt my pain, and I was in awe of his compassion. Our journeys in life had been similar.

That afternoon passed so quickly. It was sundown, and we hadn't stopped talking. Even in the shadows, I felt his light. My eyes drank in each line on his face, mesmerized by his smile and captivated by the way his eyes warmed my soul. I didn't want to move from where we were sitting, as if that would awaken me from my dream. In his presence, I felt at home. Curled up on his couch, I was where I belonged. I had finally come home, and sharing my heart with him reminded me of a fire burning, warming my soul from the chilling winter wind.

Later we dressed for dinner and drove to Red Lobster, where I hardly touched my food. After dinner, we returned to his place, and it was early morning when we finally decided to say goodnight. I stayed in his guest room upstairs, yet I felt close to him. The next morning, it felt wonderful to wake knowing I was there with him.

As I look back over those first few days with Richard, they remain the most precious memories of my life with him. It is difficult to recreate them in writing. But they're here in my heart, and tears easily flow as I remember how dearly and deeply he has always loved me. I knew it long before he said the words.

That morning, Richard shared his innermost feelings with me. The night before, after we said goodnight, he closed his bedroom door behind him. Since the moment we met, he'd felt a rush of emotions swelling into a river of love. Wanting to feel me close again, he finally drifted into a restless sleep only to awaken.

I'm in love with her, he thought, "*but I can't take on six children, seven with my own.*" And yet, he said the love he felt went beyond physical desire and any love he had experienced before. Richard was torn between his love and reality. But later that night he said, in his dream as if someone spoke to him saying, "Your love is not a love of this world, and this love will carry you through difficult times. You need only trust in your feelings."

As he spoke, gently I touched his hand. He turned to me and unexpectedly held me close as though he would never let me go.

Then softly he whispered, "I love you."

My heart stood still. I found refuge in his warm embrace. As broken wings of a bird open and take flight, my soul soared and drifted into another realm, and I felt the heavens open and rejoice. I felt his heart beating, his breath upon my hair, and his hands gently wiping away my tears, and my soul wept.

Richard wanted to marry me. He didn't want to wait, since I would have to return to Mexico in a few days and we would be separated. I can't say that reason was with me. I can't say that I made a sound and wise decision when I agreed to get married as soon as possible. But I can say that later my daughter told me for the first time she felt like she had a home and family when I did.

That morning, we knew we could not wait. We both weighed

our options and knew that if I remained in Mexico, more than likely the court would rule in Bobby's favor. Bobby was clever. He knew how to manipulate the systemt, and because I had taken the kids into a foreign country, it didn't matter whether it was in their best interest to remain there. Bobby claimed he had no assurance I would ever allow him to see them or bring them back into the United States. Our hearing was scheduled in January, and I really felt certain I would lose.

Yet, I was happier than I had ever been, and on Christmas Eve, holiday music played throughout his house as Richard prepared dinner for his mom, dad, and siblings. If they were shocked by our engagement, they didn't say a word; instead, they were happy for us.

Richard's mother and father had also been born in the Mormon Colonies, and Richard spent most of his youth there. He knew my family, and even though I was much younger than Richard and therefore did not know him, I knew his family.

Monday morning, Richard took me to the mall. He wanted to buy me a ring. We went inside Helzberg Diamonds, and there was one that I fell in love with.

Once he purchased the ring, he asked for my hand, right there in front of the salesclerk, and I whispered in his ear, "Now this isn't exactly what I would call romantic. Can't you find somewhere else to slide that ring on my finger?"

Without hesitating, he swept me out of the store, dancing through flocks of Christmas shoppers. He guided me to a more romantic place … in between racks of clothing in Dillard's department store.

Bedazzled by his overture of rapture and romance, I looked around. "How appropriate," I said. "Now that we're alone, hidden behind women's intimate apparel, how could any other place be more romantic?" I giggled with girlish laughter while Richard took my hand in his, placed the ring on my finger, and gently kissed my lips.

We must have been in a world of our own that day, because it didn't enter our minds that someone else might think we were a little too hasty in our decision to marry, but the bishop did.

As soon as we arrived home, Richard called his bishop to ask him if he would marry us that evening. Without knowing all the details, the bishop gave us the hour to be at his home. The only suitable dress I had with me was one of black lace. Knowing that black isn't exactly what one should wear to her wedding; I hastily gave the dress a blessing.

We arrived on the bishop's doorstep at eight p.m. The moment he heard when we met, he said, "What do you mean you've only known each other for three days?"

Before the ceremony, he sat us both down to give us a Bishop's Counsel. He sat behind his desk, and we sat across from him. Carefully, he opened his book, as if to stall this marriage for a few more precious moments, but no matter what he said, each time he would roll his eyes around in complete circles. Exasperated, he simply closed his book exclaiming, "Are you sure about this?" Then waving his arms he said, "Of course you must know what you're doing."

Richard was fifty-four and I was thirty-nine. *That's old enough, isn't it?*

But I'm sure he was thinking, age *doesn't have anything to do with it.*

Knowing that we weren't about to change our minds, he led us into his living room. Standing before him, we exchanged our vows.

The bishop and his wife gave us both hugs and said they were happy for us, but I would have loved to remain behind as a fly on the wall to hear their conversation once we closed their front door. Without any fanfare, we simply drove away.

The following day, I called my mother. She was still visiting with my sisters in Salt Lake City, and when I first told her that I was married, she said, "You're kidding me, aren't you?"

When I said no, she handed the phone over to my sister. I could hear her say, "Janice is playing a game with me. Tell her it isn't funny."

My sister Marsha immediately grabbed the phone and said, "Janice, you're not really serious, are you?"

When I said yes, she laughed and said, "I don't believe you."

Several times I tried to convince her I really was married. She just couldn't stop screaming, "No you're not! You couldn't be."

Finally, I realized how crazy I sounded, and so I said, "Don't panic, Marsha, of course I'm just kidding."

We said good-bye and I hung up. Richard walked into the room and asked, "How did it go?" I told him they wouldn't believe me, so finally I agreed with them and said we really weren't married.

A few hours later, I called my sister back and told her not to say a word, but just listen. I explained to her how I felt and what had happened between Richard and me, and that yes, we were married. There was a long silence at the other end of the phone. This time, Marsha believed me.

Stunned, she didn't say a word until I said, "It's okay, I know how you must feel, but just tell Mom for me."

A few days later, Richard and I flew to Salt Lake and talked with my mother and sisters in person. It took my mom a while before she could talk without crying. My mother had witnessed many years of my pain and heartache, and I know she thought I was making another mistake—until she spent some time with us.

I can only imagine what this must sound like as my words are read, and if my daughter was saying this to me, I would grab hold of her and freeze her until she was thirty. I don't know that relationships like this happen very often, but without a doubt, Richard was brought to my path to love and stand beside me and help me through the difficult years to come.

15

Complexities of Blending Families

My spinning world only grew more bewildering.
When two hearts joined together as one combined a family of many.

My happiest memories begin with Richard, but they are bittersweet in that we both had troubled children. It started with Justin. The day before Richard and I were married, I called my children. They seemed okay with it and were excited to move back to Arizona. They stayed with their dad until the end of the holidays, and then we went to bring them home.

When we drove into our driveway, Justin refused to get out of the car.

"I hate you, Mom!" he screamed over and over again.

Justin didn't waste any time in telling me how angry his dad had been the day before, "and he took it out on us," he said.

"You never cared about us," Justin screamed, "and you're the one that's trying to destroy my dad. He's really sorry, but you won't give him a second chance."

"A second chance, Justin? I gave your dad fifteen years' worth of chances."

"But you didn't try hard enough," he said.

"This is insane, Justin. Your dad and I have been divorced for nearly two years, and you didn't have a problem with that before, so why now?"

I wanted an answer from him, but he wouldn't give me a reasonable one. Justin's attitude threw me. He'd lived with his dad long enough to know exactly why I left him. He had spent time with him during the summer. He was there when his dad married his deceased uncle's wife just months after our divorce was final. He saw how quickly that marriage dissolved, and his dad had already remarried soon after his last divorce. And Justin was blaming me?

For a moment, Justin almost seemed repentant, until angrily he said, "Why did you marry him? Richard doesn't want us. He'll get rid of us as soon as he can."

Pleading just one more time, I said, "You don't even know Richard, why won't you give him a chance?"

I can't speak for Justin even to this day, but the word *betrayal* rings true. He felt that he was betraying his father by staying with me,

After hours of pleading with Justin, I called Bobby to explain the situation, and the first thing he said was, "Can you blame him?" I don't think Bobby's wife was happy about it, but Justin went to live with his dad anyway. This was only the beginning of the unraveling of my family.

Later that afternoon, when Richard called his daughter, April, she laughed. She couldn't believe it. When we picked her up, she just stared at me.

Once we were all together, Richard genuinely wanted my kids to feel welcome, and I wanted a good relationship with April. He took an interest in how the kids were feeling and in what they wanted to do.

In January, Richard and I attended the custody hearing, and even though Bobby tried to convince the court that I was an unfit mother, the fact that I was living inside the country satisfied the judge. The judge also informed me that had the children not been living in Arizona prior to the hearing, he would have ruled in favor of my ex-husband.

Bobby and I were awarded joint custody, but I was the custodial parent. Then as soon as the judge ordered Bobby to make his $400-a-month child support payment (for all six children) Bobby stormed out of the courtroom vowing that I owed him and he would never pay me, which he never did.

In the months that followed, I noticed how quickly my kids were changing. They really were growing up. They weren't children anymore, and each searched for his or her identity. I don't know that they ever knew what that meant while stepping into a new phase of their lives. Their teenage years drastically changed our family, and we were already barely holding on.

By this time, things weren't going well for Justin. Even though he denied it, he didn't sound happy when we talked on the phone. I knew he was having problems, but he wouldn't talk to me about them. I know living with his dad brought back the same anxiety he had suffered from in the past. In time, he was failing in school.

I spent time with Justin whenever I could. When he had a basketball game, I went to watch, and we would spend time together on weekends. I knew he wanted to live at home with me—he seemed so vulnerable—but he had his pride, and it was hard for him to admit he had made a mistake.

Then there was April, Richard's troubled twelve-year-old daughter who had been living with him at the time of our marriage. She wasn't ready to share him with six other children or me, and she had become increasingly difficult for her father to control.

Richard was already having severe problems with her long before he married me. He was unable to date anyone without his daughter interfering and causing problems for him.

I spent time alone with April to get to know her. I have fond memories of afternoons shopping at the mall trying on similar clothes and modeling in front of the mirror, giggling like two teenage girls.

In spite of her negative behavior, I saw another side to April, and she was a compassionate young girl. She had a sense of humor that could lighten anyone's mood, but she also had layers of hurt and resentment. She was angry with both her mother and her father. She had been for years, and she certainly wasn't ready to surrender and allow my children or me into her life easily either.

One moment she was sweet and innocent, laughing and kind, but the instant her mood changed—watch out. When she didn't get her way, the walls in the house vibrated and doors were broken as she slammed them back and forth.

I knew my children were hurting, but I couldn't reach them, and they rebelled in every way possible—from taking the car without permission to staying out all night drinking and running with a wild crowd.

Then Darinn wanted to live with his dad. First he said he just wanted to be with Justin so his brother wouldn't be alone, but I also knew he didn't feel like he belonged in our home either.

Darinn and Justin lasted about nine months at their father's. Even though Bobby refused to send Justin home, Darinn was free to leave anytime. But once he returned, I wasn't about to leave Justin behind.

I waited until Justin was in school one morning before I went to see him. I took him out of class and demanded that he tell me *why* he wouldn't leave his dad.

"You're miserable, Justin, why do you stay?"

Justin looked down at his feet but he wouldn't answer me. "I'm okay, Mom," he finally answered.

"No, you're not," I said. "I want you out of there. I want you home where you belong."

Still, Justin wouldn't budge. When I confronted him with his smoking and possible drug use, he denied it. I looked at his clothing. My heart ached to see this young boy dressing in extremely baggy jeans that two of him could fit inside; they weren't even around his waist. Chains were hanging from pocket to pocket while his pants dragged below his waist and made a puddle around his feet.

With tears in my eyes, I demanded to know, "Why do you want to dress like this?"

He answered, "I'm a skater, Mom, and this is how we dress."

His hair was shaggy, and he looked more forlorn and lost than any child I had ever seen.

Adamantly I told him, "You're coming home with me, whether you want to or not."

Then he said, with tears in his eyes, "I can't, Mom, you'll get in a lot of trouble if you try. Dad has custody of me, and he will have you thrown in jail if you take me."

"That's not true," I said.

"Yes it is, Mom. I signed a piece of paper telling the judge that I wanted to live with my dad."

"Why would you do that?"

"Because I felt bad," he said. "No one likes Dad. You don't, and Rob and Nathan will hardly talk to him."

"That's not your problem, Justin," I answered.

With resignation he said, "But Dad cries all the time, you just don't know how sad he is."

Pain twisted my heart. Overtaken with guilt, I felt responsible for all that had happened. For many months, Justin had been more afraid of the trouble he would cause me than the hostile situation he was living in.

I told Justin he had been lied to, but just the same, I felt panic. I left Justin at school and told him to wait for me; he was not to go home. Quickly I drove to the county courthouse and searched through every record concerning Bobby and me.

I found more than I anticipated. I ran across divorce decrees in Bobby's name. In disbelief, I stared at the records.

This was the first time I knew that Bobby had been married six times before me!

I was startled by the information staring me in the face, but I didn't have time to think about it. I had to make sure I was still Justin's custodial parent. I found the document Justin was referring to, but amazingly, it had been forgotten. A date for a hearing had never been set, and the line for the judge's signature was blank. I hurried back to school. I took Justin out of class and told him we had nothing to worry about.

Justin didn't pack his clothes that day. We immediately left for Tucson, and later on I returned to gather his belongings.

Perhaps all I needed to do was stand my ground from the beginning and refuse to budge an inch. Perhaps I should have ruled my children with as much force and discipline as possible, but I didn't. I didn't know how to—and even if I did, I might not have been any more successful.

Still, I did as I had been taught to hold my troubled family together. Every Sunday, we attended church, and I tried to get them to attend church activities during the week.

At first we didn't have problems with church attendance, but in time my kids felt threatened. They didn't fit in. They felt rejected since we weren't the picture-perfect family.

"This just isn't acceptable," I screamed day after day. "What do you expect parents to think, Darinn, when you show up to church with an earring in your ear?" Even though they tried hiding it, I could smell cigarette smoke on them when they came home. "Now you'll never be included with your Mormon friends," I cried.

When Darinn first came home with a pierced ear, I thought I

would die. How was I going to explain that to my family? Later, not only did he have a pierced ear, his leg boldly displayed a magnificent dragon tattoo.

In reality, the boys felt rejected from the mainstream. And what they were taught in their young-adult classes didn't make them feel any better about themselves. In fact, they felt worse. Everything that had ever happened to them was either in the form of physical, mental, or sexual abuse.

My kids weren't products of a picture-perfect family, but I felt pressure to raise them that way. They were children raised in violence, and now they had a voice and the ability to exert their will. I was at a loss in knowing what I could do.

While they were trying to find their real identities, I tried forcing one on them that had never worked for me either. My children didn't fit the mold; they were different, and nothing I did changed that. They needed unconditional acceptance without fear of rejection or blame, and they certainly didn't need to feel any additional guilt. They needed counseling and a tough-love approach. What I needed was help in understanding their behavior and how I could deal with it more appropriately.

Robby and his friends had desert parties where they would stay out all night drinking. Many times he came in at four in the morning so intoxicated he couldn't make it up the stairs to his bedroom.

Sometimes Darinn didn't come home at all. When he did, he slept during the day. He had no direction in life, and he didn't care. He was looking out for himself and doing whatever he felt like doing.

One afternoon, during a heated argument to get him off the hook for his drinking, Robby shifted my attention to his brothers. He swore that he knew Darinn and Justin were also using drugs. As soon as Justin walked in the front door, I started in on him.

"I want the truth," I said. "Are you smoking pot?"

The look on Justin's face was a dead giveaway. Justin wasn't as adept at lying as Darinn was.

In time, something I could never have imagined happened: Darinn stopped coming home. He lived on the streets with a rough crowd.

It wasn't just my older kids who were facing a crisis in their lives. The atmosphere, the rebellion, and the lack of control had a ripple effect on my younger children. Nathan was only eight years old and had already tried smoking with one of *his* friends.

The straw that broke the camel's back came one afternoon when Darinn returned home after a four-day hiatus. The moment he walked in my front door holding on to his beyond baggy pants so he wouldn't trip on them, dirty and blurry-eyed, I hit the ceiling. First he tried to walk past me. I wasn't about to let him walk out of the room without getting the answer I wanted from him.

He mumbled a few incoherent words. Although I knew that he was high, I didn't stop. He tried to go around me, and I grabbed on to him. He dragged me as far as the garage. I was still screaming at him to stop when he exploded. First he shoved me away from him and I fell to the floor, and then I watched in horror as he went wild. Our garage looked bombed out as he pounded his fists through the drywall from one end to the other. He was completely out of control, and the rage I saw in him scared the life out of me. His fists were bleeding, but that didn't stop him. Only seconds had passed before I ran into the house to call 911, but before I had a chance to pick up the phone, Darinn ran out into the streets. He jumped over a retaining wall, fleeing into the desert.

Scared for him, for me, and for my other children, who stood by in horror watching their older brother, I put my head in my hands and wept, crumbling into a heap on the cold garage floor.

That night I paced the floor. Every few seconds I peeked out the window in the hope that he would return. With tears of agony flowing, I wept. The night was still when finally I fell to my knees and prayed for his safety.

I wasn't alone in my living room that night. God's angels were with me. Shimmering outlines of bright light surrounded me, and I felt the warmth of their luminosity. As I continued to pray, mentally I could see a host of angels protecting my son. They weren't like the angels that stayed with me. These spiritual beings were large in stature, exuding power and protection.

I was comforted, but my fear was greater than my ability to trust in the powers of angels. I knew I needed to let go and let God, but the night was too dark. Shadows frightened me, and the thought of Darinn overdosing or being in other danger was a real threat for me.

A few days later, friends of Darinn told me that he was now hanging out with some pretty tough kids from the south side of Tucson. He wasn't playing around with small stuff; this time, he was using crack cocaine and stealing cars.

Darinn was the one of my children who frightened me the most. He was the one who had borne the brunt of his father's vicious verbal abuse. In his father's eyes, he never did anything right. Since he was a small child he had been ridiculed, and according to his father, he was certain never to amount to anything. His wounds went deep, and I knew how terribly hurt he was. But how was I to stop him from hurting himself?

Finally, Richard convinced me there was nothing I could do. Exhausted, with my eyes swollen and my head throbbing, I went to bed. The following morning, that horrible knot was still in my stomach. Days went by, and still no word from Darinn.

I filed a runaway report on Darinn, and then several weeks later he finally came home on his own—but he didn't stay. By then, I had no doubt that Darinn had gone beyond marijuana; hard drugs had become his way of life. Off and on he would show up at the home of a friend who knew Justin. That's when Justin started staying away from home also. By then, I wasn't just afraid for Darinn, I was angry as hell with him. He seemed magnetic—what he did, the others did too, and Justin was one of his favorite little cronies.

Searching through the Yellow Pages, I made phone calls to different drug-treatment centers. We didn't have health insurance; therefore, none of the treatment centers would agree to help us unless I paid cash. Unable to afford the cost, I really felt helpless.

April wasn't involved with substance abuse, but her temper and lack of discipline continually wore me down. She fought with Lynsey. She resented Nathan and Westin.

"What else can possibly go wrong?" I asked Richard one night after a heated argument with April. He sadly shook his head. He didn't have any answers either. We had yet to find a solution that actually worked. Grounding her and taking away privileges or possessions had no affect on her.

The only thing I can say for certain is that Richard really did love me. Physically and emotionally I wasn't well, and he was more concerned about me than anyone else. I battled severe depression, along with other autoimmune disorders that only worsened with the stressful problems I continually faced.

At night, Richard would hold me tight. I was terrified of slipping into that deep, dark, and terrifying black pit. He was frightened for me. Unless I stabilized, my children wouldn't either. During the day, he would take me with him, and often we found quiet places to sit and talk. Being with him was healing. The energy around him was calm, and he always reminded me of his love.

16

Prescription Drug Abuse, My Way of Coping

Sometimes you have to hold on until the storm is calm and the sun warms the earth again, and during troubled times the only solace you will find is prayer. Praying for strength, knowing God sends angels to watch over you.

With each passing day, Richard became increasingly concerned. He took the keys to my car and begged me to see another doctor. He saw many changes in my behavior that contributed to my problems, in part due to the medications I was taking. But as my depression worsened, my doctor only increased my dosage of Prozac and continued prescribing Ambien and Xanax.

One particularly bad day, Richard took me into our bedroom, and sitting me down on our bed, he said, "Janice, let me take over with the discipline."

My heart froze.

"No way," I said.

Holding his hand up he said, "Hear me out—"

"No, I'm not going to step aside; you can't do it, Richard. You don't know how to do it any better than I do."

"They are walking all over you, Janice. You've got to stop protecting them, and you need to follow through with some pretty tough consequences."

"Right," I said, "as if you know how to do that."

I reassured Richard that I could handle the situation. With runaway reports filed on both Darinn and Justin, I finally found a drug-treatment center that would take them. That solved one problem, but I had many more to face. First I had to locate Darinn and Justin, and then I had to face the fact that I was unable to adequately care for Nathan, age eight; Lynsey, age seven; and Westin, age six. I asked my mother for help, and she offered to keep them for a while.

The day Richard drove away with them, I knew I would never see sunlight, feel laughter, or experience joy again. Today the haunting memory of their little pleading faces still reminds me of their pain. They didn't understand why they had to leave, and Nate could only ask, "Mommy, what did I do wrong to make you send me away?"

One afternoon in late May, the police contacted me. They had found both Justin and Darinn inside a trailer house within miles of our home. I asked them to take both boys to Cottonwood, the drug-treatment center. I met them at the facility, and both were admitted that afternoon.

Even though Robby refused treatment as an inpatient, he did attend the family sessions. During these sessions, he couldn't help but share his pain. Being able to talk about it gives way to feeling what you tried so hard to forget. Robby wasn't ready for healing any more than his brothers, but all the same, they were affected by what went on during this time.

As soon as the school year ended, April went to stay with her mother, and for the first time part of my family was in counseling together. I was amazed at what I was learning about my children, but the family sessions with my boys were almost too painful as they finally allowed me to see everything through their troubled eyes.

One of the counselors explained that it might be difficult for me to hear my boys express their pain. "It won't be easy," she said. "They are angry with you as well as with their father." But nothing quite prepared me for the agony I felt. Listening to them tell the story of their childhood abuse was one of the most excruciating experiences of my life.

Unable to escape reality, I felt the faces of my growing boys rip my heart apart. Is this what I had done to them? Between bouts of agonizing remorse and unforgiving anger, I would leave the center and go home wounded and hurting, crawl into bed, and cry myself to sleep.

The next day, I returned to help them face their anger. Because of what they were learning about addiction, Darinn and Justin accused me of having a chemical dependency. *How absurd,* I thought. I didn't have a chemical dependency—mine were "prescribed" medications. I denied it; in fact, I resented both of them for saying it.

I honestly believed that I wasn't to blame for the medications I was taking. Bobby was responsible, and my boys were. Could they not see what their choices were doing to all of us? Truthfully, I hated the fact that I didn't have a life. I felt like I was walking around in shock amid the ruins of what I once believed was my family.

I just wanted the pain to go away. I wanted to feel better. I hated waking in the morning with a knot in my stomach. I hated existing in a world of darkness, and I hated myself as a woman and a mother more at that moment than at any other time.

I didn't have any control over my life, and the only skills I had to change my life were the old ones that hadn't worked in the past.

It was important that we receive counseling, and I hoped Bobby would accept responsibility for the damage he had caused.

Both Darinn and Justin asked him to attend the family session, but he chose not to, and this was a tragic mistake. They needed this healing time with their father before it was too late. I was angry with Bobby. He had failed me in every way, but I couldn't help but be angry with myself also for the expectations I still had of him.

Even without their father's presence, the family sessions were an important aspect of the treatment program. I will also have to say that placing Darinn and Justin in a safe facility was more important for me than it may have been for them. They didn't ask for help. Every chance they had, they tried running. Once they were successful, but within days both were located and returned to the facility.

Perhaps one of the most vivid memories I have of the family sessions began one morning when the room was filled with victims and their families. Some of the inpatients were teenagers and others were close to my age, but the one thing they all had in common was their inner pain.

One young man, who was close to six feet tall, even stood on a chair because he needed to feel larger than his father had once seemed to him when he was beaten as a child. The scene was almost unbearable for me. Everyone inside that room felt this young man's anguish and need to take back his power.

Witnessing the intense emotions from this twenty-six-year-old man brought to life my children's pain. Through him, I saw my children; vivid memories of little boys standing in their bedroom while their father beat them with his weight belt left me in agony.

Allowing painful childhood memories to surface is essential to recovery. It's important, at any age, that victims own their power, and that means taking it away from the one who took it from them.

For the first time, I was feeling my deepest feelings with my children. Together we cried. We expressed our innermost feelings of anger and deep emotional pain.

Heartbroken from the severity of my older boys' problems, I was forced to face reality. What part had I played? What had that role done to my children?

In my darkest hours, I reached out to hold on to a sense of security, but I was sinking deeper into depression, and my children's pain was a current stronger than I could withstand. I wasn't ready to face my children's demons before I conquered mine.

The time for Justin and Darinn's release from Cottonwood came all too soon. Richard and I had already decided that we would move from our neighborhood. We found a perfect place to build a home. We hoped that being in a different environment would help them choose different friends.

Unfortunately, after we moved, nothing really changed. Darinn ran away from home again, and Justin just found new friends with the same habits. Even though he was attending school, he was failing most of his classes.

Several months after we moved into our new home, Nathan, Lynsey, and Westin came home. They had been with my mother for the past school year and anxiously wanted to be in their own home. At the same time, April's mom insisted we take her also. I wanted time alone with my children, but that wasn't to be, and the moment April walked through our front door, I knew our problems were only starting over.

April was worse than she had been in the past. Because she was forced to move in with us, she felt angry and resentful. I don't blame her. She felt rejected by her mother, and rather than adjust, April bitterly fought with Lynsey and Westin.

To make matters worse, April's mother and grandmother criticized me and interfered with my disciplinary measures. They sided with April, which only reinforced her negative behavior in my home.

To add to our problems, Richard and I were worried Nathan would follow in his older brothers' footsteps. He was failing almost every subject in school, and he wanted to drop out. Nathan was an angry child. He was so young when I left his father, but not once in his short life had he felt safe. The reasons for our divorce didn't seem to matter as much as what the abuse and my emotional illness did to him. He was undergoing counseling, but he resented anyone who wanted to help him. Finally, he was placed in a special program for students at risk, but in time we realized that even this did not help him.

Darinn was still a runaway. I had no idea where he was, and I worried about him night and day. Little bits of information made its way through his old circle of friends, and the news about Darinn wasn't anything I wanted to hear. Several of his friends were now serving time in prison, and I felt it was only a matter of time before my wild child joined them.

Rob turned seventeen that summer. He was drinking with his friends almost every night, and he wouldn't get out of bed long enough to look for a job. Sick of pleading with him and allowing his problems to get me down, I warned him that if he didn't change, he would have to leave.

The morning I finally said, "I've had enough." I awakened him. I told him it was time for him to leave our home. I'll never forget the look on his face when he said, "Where will I go, Mom? You can't do this to me."

Later that week, I drove Robby to Mesa and dropped him off at his dad's. Bobby agreed to keep him while Rob looked for a job or until he found a place to live. But Bobby's new wife refused to allow Rob into their home. Soon after I returned to Tucson, Robby was forced to leave his father's home. He slept in his dad's car, and during the day he looked for a job. Bobby helped Robby find an apartment once he found a job.

Darinn contacted me for the first time in over a year and wanted to come home, but I knew that nothing had changed with him. Because of the problems with my other children, I couldn't let him move in with us.

My sister agreed to let Darinn live with her. He came by the house for a short period of time before he left for Salt Lake City, and I hardly knew him. I felt my heart break when I saw him. Drugs had completely changed my son.

After living with my sister for nearly a year, Darinn needed to be on his own. His drug habit was just as bad in Salt Lake as it had been in Arizona.

Robby was living in an apartment by that time, and so Darinn moved in with him. This only made the situation worse for Robby, who was barely making it on his own. Darinn didn't work; instead, he stayed at home stoned out of his mind. It didn't take him long to make friends with other addicts, and this made Robby's life a living hell.

Richard's advice to Rob was to throw Darinn out, but that was easier for Richard to say than for Rob to actually do. Between me and my children, not one of us had the ability to keep ourselves safe from the destructive behavior of others.

I had been using and abusing prescription drugs for nearly three years, but when the medication no longer seemed to work, in desperation I combined alcohol with my sleeping pills. Since any use of alcohol was against my religious beliefs, I became a closet drinker. Late at night—or any other time of the day—I huddled underneath my clothes where no one would find me and drank.

Anyone looking from the outside may have thought, "What is wrong with that woman?" as if I could wave a magic wand and dissipate my illness or just snap out of it.

But I couldn't.

Then I met Sheri. She moved into our neighborhood the same time we did. We became friends. Since Sheri was a nurse, she immediately knew I was overmedicated.

Sheri also found me in my bathroom with a razor blade, trying to get the courage to cut my wrists. She talked to Richard and then called a friend of hers, a psychiatrist, and made an appointment for me.

I started therapy with Dr. Johnson several times a week. He started me on a lithium treatment for bipolar depression but still prescribed Ativan for me. Richard joined me in therapy. For obvious reasons, I couldn't do anything about the interference and problems created by April's mother and grandmother, but Dr. Johnson strongly recommended Richard be more aggressive.

As if things couldn't get any worse, several months later I received a phone call. Darinn and Rob had lost their apartment, and they needed a place to stay temporarily. Since I was still trying to save them, I allowed them to move in with me.

The night Darinn brazenly traipsed back into my home; he didn't care what he brought with him. He really didn't have an ounce of remorse or responsibility in his bones. Although I warned Darinn and Rob about the consequences if they didn't find work and move out soon, Darinn didn't hear a word I said, and apparently neither did Robby.

Darinn brought drugs into our home. Rob had his drinking problem, and since he now had a roof over his head, he wasn't motivated to find work.

Nathan ditched school. During parent/teacher conferences, I was made aware of the possible dangers Nathan faced, but Nathan wasn't listening to anyone. He was running with friends who had a negative affect on him, and his attitude completely changed. He wanted to dress just like his older brothers. He wanted to run with a crowd just like his brothers'.

They smoked, so why couldn't he? They had dropped out of school, so why shouldn't he?

Heartsick and filled with anguish, I believed that I had failed.

One by one, I lost all of my children as they reached adolescence. The first three were close in age, but Nathan was four years younger. I had hopes for him. I felt that it would be different for him. He was only five when I left his father.

With each child who slipped away, I wallowed in guilt. I couldn't move beyond it. I felt so responsible for what Bobby and I had done to our children that I felt it was my obligation to save them. I would have given anything to turn their lives around. Even though I knew my behavior was irrational, I couldn't relinquish the control I foolishly convinced myself I had.

Many times I told myself, *"If I just help them this time, they'll get on their feet"*. I always felt there was something more I could do that would make a difference. Richard didn't agree with me, but he couldn't force me to see things his way.

I was doing the best I could. I was living the only way I knew how, and it was as unhealthy with my children as it had been with Bobby. I lacked the skills necessary to enforce consequences and to step outside the drama of each angry child, but I was also still emotionally healing. I can only imagine how different our lives would have been had I been healthy enough to be their parent.

Recovery is a family matter. It wasn't enough that I received professional counseling, my children also needed a safe place to vent their anger and express emotions, a place that offered information, love, and support.

Tough Love is an organization that offers help to parents with troubled teens. While I didn't have the ability to implement family rules and follow through with tough-love consequences, another parent can. There is support between families, and most of all, education.

If you are a parent, don't wait until it is too late. I lived my life doing the best I could, but what about my children? What choices did they have? While they may not have had choices while in their youth, when they grew up the story changed, and so did their behavior.

---

* More information about Tough Love is given in the back of the book.

17

My Intervention

We all have angels guiding us …. They look after us.
They heal us, touch us, comfort us with invisible warm hands ….
What will bring their help? Asking. Giving thanks.
—Sophy Burnham

One weekend, we took a trip to Mexico, and while horseback riding I was thrown from my horse, breaking bones in my shoulder that required surgery. It was too far to travel back to Arizona, so I had my surgery done at a local hospital.

My drug abuse increased considerably during this time. Along with pain medication, my doctor in Mexico prescribed more Ativan for me. By then, I had quite a supply of the drug, but even that wasn't enough.

Finally, it was time to go home, but just before I left Mexico, I had my doctor prescribe extra medication for me. I picked it up from the pharmacy and stashed it away. When Richard arrived at my mother's, he was concerned. My mother told him I was taking a lot of pills and sleeping more than I should. Since Richard was aware of the problem I'd had with pills before the accident, he went through my makeup bag and counted how many pills I had with me.

We left Mexico the following day, and several weeks later, he overheard me asking the receptionist in my doctor's office for a refill of Ativan.

"What are you doing?" he asked in the middle of my conversation.

"I'm out of medication, and I just need a refill," I answered.

He shot back, "Tell her you don't need it."

"What?" I exclaimed, putting my hand over the receiver so the receptionist wouldn't hear him. "Of course I do."

Richard promptly took the phone away from me and told the receptionist, "Don't give her a refill. She still has enough pills that she brought with her from Mexico to last her throughout the month."

What he didn't realize is that I had already taken the every last pill I had. The first night without it, I lay awake all night. Restless and nervous, I was exhausted by morning.

To make the situation worse, early on a Monday morning a police officer appeared at my door. Bobby's family didn't have my telephone number, and they needed to get hold of me.

The officer simply said, "Here is a phone number—it's urgent that you call."

I hurried and dialed the number. John, Bobby's brother, answered the phone.

"What's wrong?" I asked.

He answered, "Bobby died Saturday night. He wasn't found until late yesterday afternoon in his apartment."

Nathan hadn't left for school yet. He was standing by me when I made the call. I put down the phone, turned to Nate, and said, "Your dad passed away."

His face drained of color, and then he cried, "No, Mom, it can't be true, he isn't dead."

I tried to comfort him, and briefly, he let me hold him as he sobbed, but he wouldn't hold still. He ran into his room, slamming the door behind him. After I told Richard the news about Bobby's death, he left to pick the other kids up from school. That afternoon, I watched as my children tried to absorb the news about their father. My heart ached for them. So much pain in such a short span of time, and they were still children.

Several days later, my children and I attended their father's funeral. Together we sat on the front pew in the chapel. The casket was closed, and it all seemed surreal. Inside the casket was the body of a man I hated and yet had spent fifteen years of my life with. We had children together, and they loved him.

Regardless of what Bobby had done, his children never stopped loving him, and I couldn't stop crying. I'm sure family members thought I was grief-stricken. I don't know what I was feeling, but I ached for my children, and I know I was an emotional wreck.

After the service, Bobby was taken to his final resting place, and his children looked on in bewilderment. How were they to heal without him? As the casket was lowered into the grave, emotions that I can't even explain tore at my soul.

I wanted to stand up and scream, "This isn't fair, "How can he die without making things right?" If possible, I would have dragged his body from the casket and made him face misery with me.

We returned home in the early afternoon, and later that night, I slipped into a world different from any other. It was filled with inner darkness, covering my body with a heavy blanket of terrorizing fear. My mind was entering a place that could only be described as hell.

By morning, I thought I was losing my mind, as I continued to experience paranoia and extreme agitation. I made many phone calls to my doctor telling him about my situation, but my doctor thought I was having another mental breakdown. Since I didn't have health insurance, my husband was trying to find a hospital that would take me.

That's when Belle, who had been my friend for years, felt she needed to be with me. She was not in the habit of coming very often, as we lived hours away from each other, but that day she showed up at my doorstep, and I don't know what I would have done without her. As soon as she saw me, she knew my behavior was a reaction from chemicals, and that I was not losing my mind.

Belle stayed with me during a very difficult time. Going through withdrawal after years of abusing several narcotics was frightening. I thought I was going to end up in the insane asylum and someone would throw away the key.

Knowing that a hospital was not going to admit me, Belle tried to calm me by telling me the worst was almost over.

"If you just hang on, Janice, the drugs will soon be out of your system enough for you to feel better. You're almost there."

I didn't believe her. I knew my mind was gone forever. Finally, late into the third night, a calm feeling filled my being.

"Belle," I said, "someone is here with me. I can feel them sitting next to me."

Of course, Belle didn't see anyone, but she listened. Fear and paranoia completely left me. I wasn't hallucinating or imagining— the feeling was powerful and yet loving. I felt the presence of an angelic being as a voice gently but forcefully spoke to me in a clear and calming manner.

The voice adamantly said, "*You have had time to get well. Many opportunities have been placed in your hands, but you have remained ill. It is important for your future that you fully recover. There will be changes in your life, but they are necessary.*"

I knew the message meant, "*Janice, you are going to move again.*"

I had spent most of my life packing my belongings and moving. In seventeen years, I had moved too many times to count, and I distinctly remember answering, "*Oh no, I won't. Wild horses cannot make me move one more time.*"

The voice simply said, *"Wild horses won't be necessary."*

Richard and I had talked about selling our home for some time. I was so angry the day he allowed a real-estate agent to put a sign in our front yard, but it had been there for a few weeks. I wasn't that worried about having to move.

The next day, Richard signed a contract. Our home was sold. Belle had also talked with my doctor and he authorized one last prescription of Ativan. I was to slowly taper off my medication over the next six weeks. I couldn't wait for Richard to pick up my prescription. The moment I took the first pill, it didn't take long before I felt its effects, and I slept soundly for the first time in four days.

I knew we wouldn't find another home in Tucson. Richard wanted me to take Nathan, Lynsey, and Westin and find a home in Mexico, where he thought they would be in a better environment.

I disagreed. I was frantic.

Where would my older boys go? How would they survive? In my head I came up with several wild and crazy plans, but Richard continued talking without giving me a chance to argue.

"In the meantime," he said, "I'm taking you to your mother's, and the three younger kids will stay with their cousins until you are feeling better."

I knew I needed serious help, and I was relieved that my kids would be taken care of, but I was scared. When I'm frightened, I get angry. For the first time, I threatened Richard with divorce, which wasn't a smart thing to do after I thought about it—he might welcome the idea. But he wasn't the least bit worried that I would leave him. I didn't have anywhere to go. My arm was healing, and I still had to have the pin removed. This time not only was I an emotional wreck, I was crippled.

I was so certain Richard was making a terrible mistake. He had worked hard to build his business.

What would he do if we didn't stay in Tucson? I don't know if he understood at the time how important financial stability was for me. After living for many years on welfare, the life Richard offered was one of dignity. I didn't see any good in what he was doing.

I wasn't willing or able to pack, so Richard put me in the car with my overnight bag and shipped me off to my mother's. I rode in silence with tears streaming down my face.

I wasn't happy about moving, to say the least. I left behind three troubled teenagers, and I was leaving a home I loved. What I didn't realize was that my home had become my prison, one I hardly left. My behavior was wildly unmanageable, and I wasn't about to let go of problems I couldn't solve.

All three of my younger children weren't any happier with the move. They said good-bye to their friends and reluctantly packed their own things. This was a sad day, another unhappy ending. I believe they were as frightened as I was about the future.

Still, I will always remember that in the midst of chaos and at the bleakest and most troubled times, I strongly felt the presence of angels. I knew that I was being protected in every possible way, and so were my children. When I felt frightened, light surrounded me and nourished me with love.

Today, my writing is for my children, and for all those who have been robbed of a safe and happy childhood. Someday I hope to be forgiven for the life I offered my children. In the meantime, I pray that my children will know my love runs deep for each one of them.

Robby has always been my fragile one—in him, I see myself as a child. The love in his heart, which has been shattered and almost irreparably broken, hides behind his anger and dies beneath his pain, but still it shows in his countenance and breathes upon his face.

Darinn, my son who left home before he was fourteen, was the family scapegoat, and he took it for as long as he felt he could.

Driven by his anger and blinded by his pain, he took to the streets in search of a little boy lost. I see what he wants me to see, resilience and determination, and yet my heart sees behind his face and I feel his inner pain.

Justin, bright and caring, has learned to follow and has yet to test his own strength. When I couldn't save his older brothers, I threw my heart into saving him.

Nathan, my stalwart warrior, analyzes his family and is frightened by the breakdown that he sees. He is angry that he lost a father he never got to know—he is angry with his mother because he still doesn't understand the choices she had to make.

Lynsey, strong-willed and outspoken, always has to be in control, perhaps because she felt it was her job to take care of her mother. I worry more about her than my other children. What has she learned that she will take into her role as a woman, wife, and mother?

Sweet and caring, Westin is my child of peace. He just wants to live carefree with a loving mother. He seems untouched by the turmoil in his life. He has faith and believes in many things.

18

Little Steps towards Healing

Take all the time you need to heal emotionally.
It takes a lot of little steps
to break free from your broken self.

My three youngest children stayed with their cousins, and I settled in at my mother's. Robby and Darinn moved into an apartment, and Justin stayed with a friend, which was his choice. He refused to come with us, and he refused to get help for his drug abuse.

For the first time, I had time alone, and it was exactly what I needed. My body felt like it had been through an old-fashioned washing-machine wringer. I still remember the one my mother had when I was growing up, and I felt like someone had pulled me through it.

It seemed almost ironic. After four years, I was back at the beginning, where I once moved my family to Mexico to find safety after my divorce. Somehow I felt broken and defeated all over again.

Then we found a home across the river from my mom's. My

three younger children moved back with me, and I felt well enough to begin taking care of them.

But I also worried about Justin. He was only sixteen, and I wanted him to finish high school more than anything. Several times Richard and I drove to Tucson to see him. It was quite obvious that he was still using drugs.

My choice was to force Justin home one way or another, but Richard felt if it wasn't Justin's choice, he wouldn't be willing to make the necessary changes. I tried talking to Justin, but he wasn't listening. However, he did ask for money.

I was heartsick the following day when we drove home leaving Justin behind.

"This isn't the way it is supposed to be," I said to Richard. "Justin is only sixteen; he needs to be with us."

"Janice, give him some time. I think he'll come around."

I wanted to believe him.

Even though it took Justin four months before he decided he wanted to come home, he finally did. He called me one afternoon and said, "Mom, come and get me."

I drove out alone to get my son. What I picked up later that afternoon was a son high on marijuana. His eyes were dilated, blurry and red. He was also irritable and agitated.

I searched through Justin's belongings to make sure he didn't have any drugs with him. I also made him empty out his pockets and take off his shoes. He didn't have anything he shouldn't with him, but drugs were still in his system. The drive home wasn't an easy one. Three hours after we left Tucson, he changed his mind and didn't want to go with me.

Justin began swearing and yelling at me to turn around. We had gotten this far, and I wasn't about to go back. Then Justin started fighting with me.

"I said, turn this damn car around," he screamed as he grabbed the steering wheel.

I managed to pull off to the side of the road as Justin fought for the keys.

Afraid that he might get the keys, I jumped out of the car with them. I waited for nearly an hour in the hot sun, upset and angry that he had control over me.

Finally, we made a truce.

"Give yourself time," I said. "If in several months you still hate it in Mexico, then you can go back."

Finally, he agreed.

It took time before the drugs were out of Justin's body, but Justin was true to his word. He gave up smoking cigarettes, and he quit using drugs. That fall, he enrolled in high school and studied hard. I was amazed and so proud of his progress.

Robby and Darinn struggled. This was a rough time for them, but they were also slowly learning. Neither one of them could keep a job, so soon they didn't have a place to stay. They bummed a couch off different friends. My fear has always been that they would never find stability, meaning a job and a decent place to live.

Darinn was an addict, and I had to face that fact. Nothing Richard and I did helped him. Robby made unwise choices. Sometimes he didn't think at all, he just acted irresponsibly.

Many times I wanted to rescue them, but sometimes I couldn't. When Robby had unpaid traffic fines, he spent thirty days in jail. I suffered every day thinking of the worst that could happen to him.

I didn't bail him out, even though I wanted to. While he had time to reflect upon the choices he had made, I had time to reflect on how I could help him. Finally I was able to say, "He is where he needs to be, and it is for a lesson he hasn't learned."

I then turned to prayer and asked that he be protected.

It felt like an eternity before he was released, but we both got through this difficult time. Later, he let me know he felt comforted and protected (he needed protecting from an inmate who thought he was a birdie in the window).

If there is any lesson I want to share with battered women who have children, it's this: you aren't the only one affected. Stop for a moment and realize that children witnessing abuse are traumatized. More often, they also are victims of physical, emotional, sexual, or verbal abuse. The damage can be life lasting. You are contributing to that harm by staying. There are different forms of abuse as well, such as neglect, and you are in this situation get help now. My story is not unique—perhaps different, but not less painful and heartbreaking—but I'm still living to write about it.

The road to recovery is a difficult one. It's one you take step by step, but you also must take the hand that is there to brace you, give you shelter, and help you rebuild your life. Don't wait! Don't stay! I did, and at first I realized the effects the abuse had on me, but then I realized greater heartache through my children's behavior and their pain.

My heart ached to save each one of them for years to come. If possible, I would have returned my older ones to their tender years, before they learned to walk, and I would have run the other way. If only. If only. If only. But the past no longer exists, and I can't turn back the clock.

It seemed God or the universe intervened, and choices were made for me. My hands were once again pried from the conditions in which we were living, moving me out of the country and back to Mexico. What I thought was the end of the world was a new beginning—at least it was giving me another chance to heal, a time to face reality, which I could not have done under any other circumstances.

Moving made a difference for my three younger children. When Justin returned, he stayed long enough that it made a difference for him too. It's been a long journey to healing for all of us, but that's only part of my story. It's also about perseverance, learning, forgiving, letting go, and growing. Our dark side needs to be faced, and if we come to terms with it, do the healing work and then put this energy to good use, anything is possible.

We moved from Tucson to Mexico in 2000. By 2002, I was starting to write. It felt very natural, as if this was part of my soul's journey. I had no idea what would come of the book I first wrote or how healing it would be.

Now my writing is for you, my reader. My hope is that you too can step away from darkness toward truth and light, where you will become more whole and complete, where you will also master the complexities of your own inner nature to take that decisive step toward authenticity.

19

───◦◦✦◦◦───

First Gift of Healing:
A Love So Tender

*Our happiness is measured by our capacity to deeply love, and
with the gifts of the soul every thought, every desire, and every
breath becomes a melody of devotion, until the heart is filled
with a glorious song of compassion, mercy, and understanding.*

Each morning, before I began my work, prayer was important
in helping me know I wasn't alone. Angels and guides spent
many long hours with me. In awe of such love, I felt the sun rise each
morning and warmly kiss my face. I was finding peace.

I turned a small guest house adjacent to my home into my office.
Fragrant flowers blooming outside my window spoke of new birth,
and angels, wise in their knowing, were quietly preparing me for a
long journey ahead that would start with divine teachings of healing
and clearing the path toward a journey of deeper self-awareness and
unimaginable challenges allowing me to change—to grow through
change and the ending of a life cycle.

Meditating often, I visualized colorful rays of iridescent light flowing through me—subtle, yet undeniably enfolding me in a love so tender, so merciful, and so healing. I could feel my heart opening to receive this compassionate energy, lifting layer by layer of buried pain and then slowly releasing it, allowing me to own it. It helped me to make sense of all the anger and the pain so deeply buried I had become numb to my own feelings. During this time, tears were shed, but always divine love held me tight to walk through the storm.

In time, everything was changing about me, including my physical health, my moods, my stability, and my priorities. Step by step, the healing process was bringing mind, body, and spirit into harmony, and I felt divinely guided. I no longer depended on pharmaceutical drugs for depression or anxiety or to sleep at night. This was a huge step in my recovery, because for so long drugs only helped to suppress the anger, the pain, and the feelings that needed to be faced. At first, the antidepressant was necessary. I could not have stabilized without it, but you can't continue living with unmanageable stress and think medication is going to get you through it.

Intermittently, between writing about love, forgiveness, and gratitude, I would write different chapters of my personal story. It was difficult at first. I didn't want to dig deep. I cherished the new stability I had in my life and was afraid of upsetting that balance by dragging up the past, but I also learned I couldn't prevent healing from happening either.

My writing evolved as, cautiously, I touched the tip of my inner pain. I thought I was over much of the hurt from what went before, but my unhealed wounds were still very much a part of me. My past held memories of a young girl who had failed and her life was a story of her painful choices. Nothing I said or did could change the past, and to be honest, I still loathed the reflection of shame I saw in the mirror each day.

Quickly my world began to turn from peaceful interludes into dark and stormy periods of time. As much as I didn't like what I was experiencing, I felt safe enough to walk through my past in my writing. But as this intrinsic fear continually surfaced, my body felt sick all over again. At first I felt certain I was having a relapse. Terrified that I would slip into depression's dark pit of hell, my first reaction was get myself back on medication fast.

As if it wasn't enough to deal with the highs and the lows, my children became angry because I was writing about their deceased father. To make matters worse, Richard still wasn't able to find work. Even though he spent most of his time and what money we had traveling back and forth to El Paso, work wasn't available. Deeply discouraged, I doubted everything around me. The peace I once felt disappeared into thin air.

Nerves frazzled, a few weeks later I had had enough. I stopped writing. Too many phobias were accumulating, and in the stress from a topsy-turvy external world, the past caught up with me. I realized a few things about myself that I didn't want to face; one was my exaggerated need for security, which probably had something to do with my fear of change and clinging to the past. Not only was I emotionally spent from everyone being upset with me, I had also become that pitiful woman again, and I didn't believe in myself.

My heart ached when I walked into my office knowing that I was throwing away my dream, but I was finished with my writing. Heartsick, I reacted angrily toward everyone. Then, as if I needed to prove to myself, I took a printed copy of my manuscript and burned it outside my office door.

My kids ran outside. Nathan was hysterical, and Lynsey just stared and shook her head at me. Westin tried to put out the fire.

Then Nate grabbed me by the shoulders and said, "Mom, you're coming with me." Being the theatrical person that I am, I said, "Nate, forget it. It's too late. I'm through with this book. Everyone is angry with me, and I can't take it anymore."

"That's your problem, Mom. You give up, and then you run to your bedroom and hide." I didn't say a word; I just listened as he continued. "If you give up then we'll all give up, but I will never forgive you for throwing away all the time you spent. You weren't here for us, you were always in your office saying you were too busy, and now you're saying it was all for nothing."

I tried to stop him from talking, but he wouldn't listen. He was too busy trying to make me listen.

Finally, he said, "Mom, its okay that you're writing about Dad." Tears welled in his eyes as he continued. "I know what he did to you, and I'm proud of what you've accomplished."

Nathan thought I had burned the one and only copy of my entire hope and dream, and he was furious with me. He wouldn't stop lecturing me long enough for me to tell him my work was still safe. In haste and a little show of theatrics, I may have burned *a* copy, but I wasn't crazy enough to burn the *only* copy!

This was healing time between my children and me. I needed to know they believed in my work as much as I did. It wasn't an easy choice to write this book in the beginning, and I was worried, not knowing how it would affect them.

It wasn't long before I received a message. Asleep and dreaming, I felt a voice say, *"Janice, before you can finish your book; you must first go through the process of deep inner healing. This is what you are doing. You can't teach what you have yet to learn."*

Instantly I awoke, but the dream didn't stop. I could hear the voice telling me, *"Fear has always been your greatest obstacle. Everything that you are facing is to help you overcome it—this will be your greatest trial."*

With this message came a glorious power of inner peace. I wasn't alone in my healing; within my being, the spark of light was still there and a love so great and powerful enfolded me in my hour of need. The words written in the Bible that say "Be still and know that

I am God" really made sense to me. They opened my eyes to see, my heart to feel, and my mind to know that I am a piece of God. Within me is this source of undeniable love, and I am linked to God. From reality to unity, we are inseparable.

I sobbed! I wept, and I cried tears of joy and sweet gratitude.

I wasn't alone or abandoned by God as I had once thought, and Richard had not made a mistake. I was exactly where I needed to be, and so were my children.

Cleaning out dusty cobwebs in my office, I returned to my desk. Over the following months, my writing continued, but it was still shallow because I held back just enough of my dark secrets to keep them safe from anyone ever knowing. Yet I knew I wasn't being honest, and I was deceiving others.

Through a twist of fate, Kitty came into my life. She offered to help me with my writing, and she tirelessly worked with me. A mutual friend gave me her contact information and we began communicating. Not only did she edit the manuscript, but we were closely bonded, and I relied on her. Without her, I never would have been able to put my life story on paper. She was the force pulling me forward when I gave up. When I was weak, she was my strength, and when self-doubt raised its ugly head, she still believed in me.

After a year of dancing around the real reason I was writing, I was ready to open my heart and write from the core of my being.

But for months I wrote with a heavy heart. Self-doubt was deeply embedded, and too many painful memories surfaced. The same quiet and soft angelic voice whispered, *"Oh, little one, if you could only see what we see in you."*

This sweet, tender, and pure love that filled my heart was overwhelming. I *felt* my inner beauty, validation, and empowerment, and I rejoiced knowing that I really was a courageous woman. This was the silver lining inside fear that had always prevented me from reaching beyond self-doubt and the illusive imprisonment of the glass bubble.

At that moment I knew the savior cared about me. Kneeling before the greatest love of all allowed me to break free from my past, the ugly dark secrets that held me back as if I had been severed from my knees, unable to stand on my own two feet. Nothing had really changed about me except I allowed love to open my heart center. In God's love, I felt spiritual healing begin. His love was doing what I had not been able to do alone.

This was the beginning of a miraculous journey and a long healing process. My writing brought every dark aspect that existed inside me into the light. You see, light is love, and although it is intangible, it is also undeniable as the greatest force within the universe. In fact, it is this very light I used for comfort and guidance, the source of all existence. It is the purified energy that sustains all living things—it is God's love, the cohesive power that aligns everything within our universe and galaxy and beyond in balance and harmony.

Once we clear away the layers that separate us from God's light and the purification of God's greatest love, our heart opens. Love then begins to radiate from this powerful, incomprehensible source, and if we allow it to expand inside the body and our minds until all darkness is filled with light, our lives change dramatically because we are changed spiritually.

Once we begin on this path toward light and love, all unhealed wounds rise into the conscious mind so that we can be in touch with how we feel, know our needs, and grow in strength and determination to create lives of greater joy

It's a process that can't be stopped. Situations will happen, people will cross our path, and whatever it is that we need to help us move forward releasing shame, guilt, doubt, and fear will occur to free us from unhealed wounds of the past.

One night, as I entered my living room, my eyes fell upon a picture of my two innocent little boys, taken when they were about four and five years old. I was stricken with grief as I remembered the sexual abuse they had suffered through. That painful incident, along with the physical and emotional abuse they endured at home, had scarred and changed the lives of my precious little ones forever. This one photograph triggered a profound feeling in me, and suddenly, in agony, I feel to my knees.

Not wanting to bear such pain, I begged for the torment to stop.

"I've already lived through this once," I cried.

Then a loving voice began to whisper: *"Yes, you did, but you still carry the pain, and now you must let it go."*

I knew that my savior had taken upon Himself a mission to be an emissary of God's light; bringing to a people of darkness and ignorance awareness, showing them a way out if they listened. It was because of His great love for the sorrows of humanity that He was willing to sacrifice His life and live true to His destiny no matter the cost. At that moment, I also felt no greater love taking my hand to walk beside me, teach me the way, and comfort me in my hour of need.

I ached to gather my little boys to me and tell them how sorry I was for not being there to protect them. Unable to turn back the hands of time, instead I felt the savior hold me in His arms. As the healing began, a soft voice whispered once again, *"You are not to blame, and you must forgive yourself and let me carry your pain."*

Day after day, as tears blurred my vision, I continued to write. Writing about my children caused a flood of anguish, sending me into a world of torment.

I lived inside my children's world as abused children. I felt the terror, denigration, and shame of my children. Abuse became real in a way I cannot explain. Writing brought it to life.

In writing about my life with Bobby, wounds opened that hadn't even begun to heal. I grieved for the woman who hid in shame. Memories of broken bones, bruises, and wounds didn't stir the anger in me; I had long since put anger to rest. But I had yet to grieve. Memories ran through me washing dreams away. Wrenching heartache left me unable to see beyond a swollen river of pain.

As my fingers typed, childhood memories surfaced, and I remembered myself as a young girl. I could still feel my sadness, and how afraid I was of criticism, but in searching through my memories not once could I find a time when I felt proud of who I am.

When the memories of childhood sexual abuse surfaced, I could not see the face of the one who was humiliating me, but I could feel the shame as he touched my body in a way that hurt and felt demoralizing. I had carried this dark secret for many years, and it had altered the direction of my life and the lives of my children. Finally, my tears began to release what I had held inside for so many years.

I wept for the little girl who was afraid to tell her mother, and I wept for the little one who felt defiled as though something was wrong with her, and I wept because I carried this memory shrouded in shame.

It was a time to be alone, and oh, how I cried. I needed to know I had done nothing for which to feel ashamed. The hurt I felt went deep, and no one could share my inner pain but me. No one could change the past, but it was time to heal something that happened over forty years ago.

The reflection in my childhood mirror was of a pretty girl, but I couldn't feel her self-worth, and my physical appearance had never been enough to take away my shame. The light of God's love healed the barrier between my heart and my soul.

When I was ready, I held the pieces of my shattered past. Truth was revealed in the face of my dark and pitiful little shadow. For many years, I had been disappointed in her, but I wasn't in need of self-pity; I was in need of self-love.

For the first time, I wept with the arms of love comforting me. I had lived my life doing the best I could, and I needed to feel compassion for the small child and the hurt she experienced at such a tender age. My tears flowed for all the things I failed to do and for the love I withheld from myself.

Then I wept for the woman who was beaten by her husband. Is there anything more shaming than that? Stripped of pride and courage and in all nakedness, I saw myself as a whimpering child.

When I had had enough, there was a lull in the storm, and I basked in the sunlight, rejoicing that it was over. But it wasn't long before another haunting memory begged my attention.

First, it began as a rough draft, but through my writing, the memory came alive in a way that had never happened before.

"I can't do this," I cried. "I'm not ready."

For a while, I even convinced myself that this memory wasn't important. *"Besides, there's no need,"* I told myself. *"The few that know won't tell."*

For weeks I agonized over a decision I would have to make. Back and forth, I argued the many reasons why I should and why I shouldn't. Then, without a doubt, I knew I would have to, and so I went back into my first chapter and made revisions.

For the first time in twenty-four years, I faced the unforgivable sin in me, the tiny unborn life I ended. Even though I knew how deeply wounded I had been, I had no idea how deep those scars really went.

During the following months, I mourned unremittingly. I grieved for the loss of this child and the guilt I had felt for so many years. A mother feels the bond with her unborn child—the love is there, the need to protect and nurture is there, it's not something she thinks about or waits until the child is born to decide whether she will love the baby.

Without a doubt, I realized that no one could judge another. When we do, we are simply seeing an unhealed aspect of ourselves. In reality, judgment isn't possible; we haven't the eyes to see beyond the surface or the understanding of other souls' life purpose. We haven't walked in their shoes.

My views of a woman's choice will always be for the empowerment of all women. We must love and honor all walks of life and understand we have differences of opinions. First we must educate and advocate birth control. We must teach and do all we can to prevent the cycle of abuse. What we sometimes forget is that a pregnancy alone does not ensure a baby will not be one more child born to a mother in poverty, unable to nurture or love, or a baby born to a mother who will commit or allow horrific acts of abuse that result in death.

Countless babies are tortured outside the womb—that is undisputed—but we must also consider victims of rape and incest and know there are legitimate reasons to terminate pregnancies just as there are wonderful reasons to celebrate the arrival of one more baby into this world.

We must also reconsider where we draw the line, as if we must either swing to the far left or swing to the far right. In the middle are those who honor all life and freedom; therefore, we can't eliminate a woman's right to decide what is right for her. But without taking into consideration all the other factors that empower women to honor their bodies and honor their God-given true nature so that they quit allowing others to victimize them, the abuse cycle continues and each child born into it suffers. By and large, the world suffers.

For far too long, women have been subjugated in different ways. We've been ruled and dominated on so many different levels that involve inequality and "free doom." On one hand, we are doomed by greed, unfairness, superiority, self righteousness and ignorance, but on the other, we free our selves with greater, spiritual awareness.

I can't change the world by myself and neither can you, but we can change ourselves. When I know better, I do better. Why would I then cause harm to myself or allow others to do me harm? If I'm no longer wounded, I won't find someone to inflict more pain through malicious behavior. One of the toughest lessons we learn is how to love ourselves and know our divine and loving nature.

Life is a puzzle. Gradually, over time, and from many of our experiences, we are given one piece at a time Clearly I saw how mine were teaching me eternal principles, and they all begin with love— loving myself enough to embrace acceptance, and loving myself enough to honor my true self.

I thought about Christ's ministry, and for a moment I saw a glimpse of myself as a small child kneeling before him. My life was an open book, and my sins had been etched in bold ink. Carefully, with love in his face, He turned each page. Lovingly, He took me in His arms. I wasn't a disobedient child.

I really understood how deeply scarred I had been for a choice I made and how guilt only continued to destroy my self-image. Remembering the church court and how it was to have been a court of love saddened me.

I truly believe the process I went through further damaged me. I had suffered incredibly. I paid the price, and when it was all said and done, I never once felt any better about myself. And for years to come, deep down I believed I deserved physical beatings and humiliation. How far had I strayed from the teachings of Christ? How far had I strayed from His love? The answer to that can only be measured to the same degree as my suffering.

If only someone had said to me, "You were raped. You don't need to be forgiven," I would have welcomed those compassionate words, but to prohibit me from participating in God's church seemed contradictory to the way Christ loved. To this day, it's still incomprehensible to me.

The tears that flowed were the nourishment I needed, and as the tide began to ebb, I felt deep inner pain wash out into the middle of the ocean. In place of sorrow, love softly played a melody in witness of my Savior's love.

Over the following days, my feet graced the floor and humility filled my heart. A love more precious than sunlight, more glorious than blooming flowers, and more beautiful than singing birds healed and cleansed my soul. It was the very power of heaven placed lovingly in my hands, with a promise that if I were to live this love and speak this love until its melody sang forth in devotion from every breath and silent prayer; my life would become a glorious symphony played on into eternity.

It wasn't long before a sweet and tender voice gently reminded me to stop running from my shadow long enough to turn around and face her, love her—that's all she really needed was to be loved. In loving her, I was no longer frightened of my own weakness; instead, I was willing to let go of fear and allow it to become my greatest force propelling me further than I had ever dared venture. I believed in myself in ways I had never dreamed of before.

From this I learned that we each have characteristics we detest and aspects of ourselves we don't want anyone else to know, but unless we can accept that negative facet of ourselves, that part we detest will never let us be who we really are.

Today, I understand that this light, God's love, has the power to reach into the very darkened corners of the heart in ways that I have never felt before. Without a doubt, no human being is so lowly, miserable, and destitute that he cannot be perfected by this one gift. I believe this divine love has the power to find its way through the hallways of the past and heal the injustices of this world.

20

Second Gift of Healing:
Forgiveness

How can I forgive when my heart is still grieving?
The answer seemed almost too impossible to believe: forgive others so
you can forgive yourself. In this, there is healing peace.

There was a time when forgiveness meant self-betrayal. If I forgave no one would be responsible for these horrific acts of brutality, and I wasn't about to let certain people off the hook that easily. What they had done was reprehensible, especially in light of the damage that had been caused to my children and me.

As much as I tried to heal my bitterness, the pain I carried begged to be remembered after so many years of abuse. Finally I quit trying to forgive. I believed God would have to understand my reasons if I never forgave the man who betrayed me, and even if I forgave him, what about the man who raped my children? I felt I had a right to be angry, and I didn't want anyone telling me that it was one of God's commandments to forgive and go on.

When I started writing this chapter, it wasn't my idea. I felt inspired to begin, but I wasn't ready to forgive—and besides, I really believed God understood my reasons and He was with me on this one. But I didn't understand the laws of the universe. I really didn't understand God at all.

In spite of my hesitation, I was willing to try. First, I learned that when Christ taught us to "turn the other cheek," He wasn't talking about staying in an abusive relationship.

In fact, had I known the devastation of domestic violence long ago, I would have fled in the beginning with the blessings and help from heaven. When the Bible tells us to forgive so that we can be forgiven, it isn't God who determines who is forgiven; in fact, God isn't the one who needs to forgive anyone. His love is unconditional, and it is something very few really understand.

Then I made a mental list of all those I thought were in need of being forgiven. If you've done the "stone-tossing" exercises, then you know what you have to do.

First you gather a basketful of small stones, and then you make a list of all those who have offended you (or feelings they caused), and then you toss a stone as far as you can for each person or situation In which you were emotionally wounded.

My list was quite lengthy, and God was right at the top.

For years I went to the temple. Inside, before people enter specific sessions, there is a waiting room where soft music is played. I would sit in that room and silently pray. With my husband at my side, I would hold his hand and beg God to bless us as a family. When my prayers went unanswered, I bargained with Him. I made sacred promises to do my part and be obedient in all things. I wasn't asking much, I just wanted God to soften my husband's heart and help him find work. But each time I left the temple and Bobby's wrath ripped welts into my children's skin or bruised my body with a broken rib, I held God responsible. He wasn't fulfilling his part of the bargain.

Next on my list, and this one was a big one: my church leaders.

I was really angry with the one who convinced me I should give Bobby another chance in the first place. I allowed him to stir feelings of guilt because I wasn't any better than Bobby. At least Bobby was a worthy member of the church (and this is important when you're adding or subtracting points), while I wasn't. I had been disfellowshipped for a very serious sin, and never once had Bobby been stripped of anything.

How could I possibly overlook the bishops and a relief-society president with whom I entrusted my soul to know what was best for me? Aware of the beatings from my husband, this woman in my ward saw the bruising on my face, and yet I was a burden to her. She just wanted me to go away and stop calling her.

I had no doubt that they failed my children and me, and I was angry. I had always been taught to stay within the church for counsel and guidance because no one outside our religion knew our values. They may guide us in the wrong direction. But what good did it do me to stay within the walls of my church?

They knew Bobby was abusive, and yet they did nothing except ignore the problem, as if that would make it go away. Perhaps they didn't know what to do, perhaps they advised me to the best of their knowledge, but that didn't change the fact that we were a family in crisis—an endangered family during those dark and frightening years.

"Be obedient, Janice, and you will be blessed." How many times had I been told that? Enough times to cause me to feel completely victimized by life itself, and enough times to really fear and resent God.

I was surprised that Bobby was third on my list, but that didn't lessen his responsibility for what he had done. Memories of the times Bobby would say he loved me after beating me so badly it hurt to be touched were bigger than life. Was I to forgive him? When I felt raped by my husband and then shriveled with shame when he touched me, was I still required to forgive him?

This little exercise of tossing stones only increased the hatred

I felt for my ex-husband. I could still hear my children screaming, begging, and pleading for him to stop hurting their mother.

Completely taken aback, I then added myself to the list.

With each wretched memory, I couldn't help but remember that I hadn't saved my children when they hid from their father or when he found them and yanked them from their place of hiding to beat them for some silly thing they had done. Sometimes I even forced them to stand still just so he wouldn't hurt them more because they ran from him.

Memories of my children searching through empty cupboards for food that wasn't there and wearing dirty clothes, because I wasn't able to wash clothes or I didn't have enough money to buy them food, tormented me.

Finally, forgiveness didn't make any sense at all. I knew that I had ultimately failed my children. I had neglected them, left them to fend for themselves, and even worse than that, I had failed to protect them. I felt disgraced as a mother. Not only had I failed my children, I had failed myself.

I wasn't angry anymore. I was so filled with sorrow for the conditions in my life that forgiving my ex-husband or anyone else for that matter seemed to be a little thing, minor and almost insignificant when I recoiled and hid from my memories of being a woman and a mother.

My anger and resentment were only beginning to surface. But was it just my ex-husband I needed to forgive? Was it my religious beliefs that had betrayed me? Although I believed the answer to those questions was yes, in my heart a voice resounded a million times: *"Janice, you are the one who can never be forgiven."*

One afternoon, I sought solace in a grove of trees along a riverbed. On horseback, I rode as far as I could along the shady riverbank, and then I stopped. My heart was heavy, and I didn't understand what God wanted from me.

"What am I to be learning?" I cried. "No more riddles. Just help me understand what it is that I must learn so that I can end my pain."

As I sat at the edge of the river, the past silenced the present. Confused, I couldn't help but feel that if I forgave all those who had betrayed me that would mean I didn't matter.

If I were to forgive, would forgiveness overshadow the importance of my sorrow? What about my children? My heart ached for the lives they lived. And this was where I couldn't forgive. Not me, not Bobby, not anyone who had a hand in shaping their destiny.

Where would I be without God's emissaries? When I needed them, they appeared. I felt their presence that sultry afternoon along the riverbed.

Let it go, the words reverberated over and again. Trust and just let it go.

"How do I do it?" I cried.

"In all things there is a reason, and as you forgive, my little one, you will feel forgiven."

That quiet afternoon, I held a ceremony. A weeping ceremony!

Tears freely poured from a heart that had known more heartache than joy.

Lost in the silent breeze, I whispered, "I am sorry for the pain I have caused my children." More than anything, I just wanted to be forgiven. I carried a burden that only increased my pain. Never once did anger or guilt resolve pain for anyone.

I dearly love my children. They are part of me; their sorrows are my sorrows and their joy is my joy (a phrase my father once said to me). And as their mother, I have never harmed them intentionally.

"You have nothing for which to be forgiven—just love your children as you are deeply loved." Those words flowed through me like a gentle stream, erasing years of guilt and taking it from my heart.

From dark clouds overhead, the heavens opened, and I felt the earth respond to my pain. Gentle summer rain fell, and tiny drops danced upon the waters. Embraced with caring love, I knew the angels understood a woman's pain. A soft breeze flowed through my hair, and for a moment, I felt peaceful. Mesmerized, I didn't dare move. Raindrops kissed my face, and my mind, in quietude, felt communion between her spirit and her Creator.

On that late, sultry summer afternoon, something mysterious happened. I was feeling whole again. Tranquility filled the air, rendering its sweet melody, while leaves gently swayed, reminding me of God's unseen power. My spirit rejoiced that afternoon because I was finally learning the value of the gifts of the soul. I understood that there is a perfection to life's existence regardless of our circumstances, and forgiveness allows us to continue forward and ever onward as the soul evolves.

Each shattered piece in my life is to always be a reminder of what happens when the heart forgets. Love lives on and can never be destroyed, but the heart needs to be free to remember.

Today, I have compassion for my ex husband. Bobby was an angry man who experienced misery and sorrow all the days of his life. I pray his soul rests in peace. I pray he knows that in spite of his atrocities against his children, they love him and they always will.

I am proud that I took all the pain and suffering he gave me and wove it into a tapestry of which I am proud.

Remembering much suffering through many years of heartache, I can also see doors that opened with an opportunity to walk away. I didn't do it the first or second or third time, which isn't unusual for a battered woman. It can take many attempts. It takes courage, a plan, and resources to escape. But the longer you stay, the greater the harm and the risk you take not only with your own life but that of your children.

The most difficult paths are filled with dark nights of the soul. There are heartaches and sorrow, loss and suffering, and yet it is through this journey that the soul opens to deeper self-awareness. As we go through our trials by fire, there is a process of awaking and the beginning of our divine nature.

Forgiveness is giving yourself permission to be the divine and loving soul that you are. It is the only "gift" that frees you from your past; allowing you to see yourself through loving, compassionate eyes.

21

Third Gift of Healing
Song of the Soul:
Gratitude

*How blessed are the hearts that sing, for life
shall bless them with inner peace.*

One morning while working in my garden, I felt the warmth
of the sun. As I basked in its comfort, my mind was aware
and conscious of what was going on around me. Golden sunrays felt
nurturing, and I felt part of the earth's spirit. This glorious ball of
fire gently faces the earth each morning, promising to be there again
tomorrow. While there are many things in life we cannot rely on,
the sun isn't one of them.

Feeling joined with the miraculous beauty of the earth wasn't my
first encounter with gratitude, and it wasn't earth-shaking, nor was I
forever changed in the twinkling of an eye, but as the days went by
I took notice. I made an effort to open my eyes and appreciate what
was happening around me.

I wasn't preoccupied by my future, nor did I live in the past. Instead I made an effort to do my part, finish my writing, and listen to my heart. Each time worry crept in, I simply remained focused on what was happening.

This was a new dawn with a new beginning for me. Just as each season gives birth to something wonderful, being grateful ushers in stillness and peace, knowing that the past doesn't exist but you are creating the future. Each positive thought combined with pure emotion, which is powerful if it is filled with joy.

On that day, I continued to change. A feeling of gratitude stayed with me, and as the sun set below the earth that evening, stars across the sky became a shimmering light as love gently fell upon my world.

Another burden lifted. My heart felt light. My world was bright, and I felt positively encouraged about everything I was doing.

Slowly I was learning to weed out doubt, thus allowing the positive energy to flow, but my dream still seemed far-fetched and so far away.

Later on, Richard and I took a trip, and while I was sitting on a sandy beach in Mexico, I asked the spirit to teach me what I was still lacking in understanding. The answer came to me by way of passionate feeling. All around me, I felt a tremendous living force guiding the universe. I could feel it in the waves as they crashed upon the shore. I felt it in the clouds as they gracefully swept across the sky.

Every living thing was working together in perfect harmony.

I felt this same energy in me, but suddenly fear surfaced. I felt the waves rolling backward, the sun spinning out of control, and then I realized this same powerful energy was in my thoughts. As long as I stayed focused with positive intent on my goal, heart and mind synchronized with no doubt. I was co-creating with God. My thoughts flowed in harmony with the universe, bringing to me situations in which my dream would manifest into reality.

Peace of mind comes when you learn to trust your instincts. This is a process, one we do if we hold ourselves, our thoughts, our feelings, and our bodies in a place of love. Then there is no end to the beauty we allow to flow into our lives.

The only way I can remain in a place of love is to feel joyful gratitude, to be grateful for this moment, to be joyfully integrated with God, and to be creative. This is the moment that is ours— nothing else. The past is decayed. It doesn't exist, and we all know tomorrow has yet to arrive. Worry plagues most of us, and the more we think about it, the more the future dims our hopes. Live in this moment with a grateful heart. Create your future with intent and positive influences. You can change everything (within your world) by directing positive energy in the direction you want to go.

It wasn't long before Richard was introduced to a man who hired him as a subcontractor on a large project. He left Mexico to work in the Mogollon Mountain area just above Payson, Arizona. Westin was a sophomore and Lynsey was a junior in high school, and after a few months we decided to move to Payson to be closer to where he was working. We both saw this job as a blessing brought to us by providence, and we felt a loving force guiding our lives.

Beneath Wings of an Angel was first published in 2004. Finally, I was living a dream and fulfilling a mission I believed in passionately. Hope survived; I spoke from my heart at fundraisers for domestic-violence organizations, in television interviews, and in auditoriums filled with high-school students.

Never have I felt so blessed in giving. Each time a student wrote to me thanking me for making a difference in her life, my heart filled with gratitude. This really is what "beautiful heartbreak" means, making something out of our sorrows, out of our losses, out of our pain.

Years of battering didn't break my spirit or destroy my dignity as a beautiful woman and a mother of pride. I thank God for protecting me and my children. No one knows our path or where our journey will take us. We will experience what is necessary for us to grow, but I know some of us are here to give light by becoming light, which light is God's purest form of love.

Today, as I write, I will count my blessings and name them one by one.

I am grateful that my past has offered many mountains for me to turn into a stairway, taking me further than I have ever dreamed.

I am grateful for the love that is in my life, my children and the times we learned to pull together, to love, to forgive, and to go on.

I am grateful for the tears I've shed, for they are nourishment to my heart, renewing hope and giving new life after storms have passed.

And in my heart, I've saved a special place for kindred spirits who have graced my life with their love and open hearts.

Rowena, my sweet friend, I see her smiling face and in my memories we're walking arm in arm, autumn leaves rustling around our feet in the cool Arizona sun.

My hand still feels her soft touch as she stayed by my side in the hospital emergency room the night I overdosed.

My most cherished and dearest friend left his earth before I could say good-bye. Softly whispered words of gratitude are sent her way; as tears glisten and fill my eyes, I long to hear her voice.

Comforted, I know her soul feels my love. She will always be remembered and revered in my choicest memories of someone who cared for me.

There is another place in my heart that sings with a continuous song of gratitude for the angels on high who wrote with me each day.

Each word of gratitude resonates with life beyond the stars, as the melody of love plays on throughout eternity. If I desire happiness, I must give another person a reason to smile; if I desire love in my heart, I must heal another with sweet and tender compassion.

Over the course of several years, the angels encouraged me to be willing to open my heart. From their teachings, I learned that in love, forgiveness, and gratitude we find the pathway to wholeness and inner peace. We learn to love ourselves and to embrace our imperfections by accepting our dark side and walking through that darkness to reveal our light.

Each gift of the soul has its own virtues. Intricately they go hand in hand, and as I wrote about thankfulness this is the message the angels shared with me: *As each day unfolds, let your heart sing. Bless all that is given for you to live. Then when evening shadows fall, you can send this gift into eternity, a glorified light with joyous strains of gratitude because your heart embraced it, your life was touched, and you lived it.*

22

A Glimpse into our Lives Today.

*In each of us is a sorrowful chant that has a harmonic quality, a
melody that goes beyond our resistance to the part of us that is in
bondage. We must free that voice, the True Self, the Divine Spark
of Life and Love, the Source of our existence, breathe of life that
nourishes and comforts and guides us through every situation.*

Beginning over ***again*** seemed impossible when everything I
worked so hard to achieve peaked soon after my first book was
released in 2004. From a successful book tour, media exposure, and
book signing events, my personal life was fulfilling. But it was also a
very troubling time within my family. The problems seemed endless
with several of my older boys challenging my ability to continue
building a strong foundation for my career. Perhaps it really wasn't
time for my success but it was the first time I really felt alive.

Living in Payson, Arizona, with Lynsey and Westin, was
enjoyable. I also kept busy traveling speaking about domestic and
teen dating violence. As time passed that year, I was also closer to
Darinn in proximity and our lives intertwined once again. After
the breakup with his girlfriend, the baby I cared for and love as one

of my own was estranged from me too. I wanted to believe my son was changing his life and my heart ached to be with this baby. I felt my only option was to file petitions with the court to establish his rights as a father, therefore; my rights as his grandmother to see my grand-baby.

But, ultimately, this back fired on me, and alienated the baby's mother further from me for several reasons. Before my son's paternity rights could be established through the court, he had to take weekly drug tests. He passed each drug screening, but before the final hearing, our attorney took me aside. Darinn had recently failed his previous drug test.

In the privacy of his office, I wept. I love this little boy, but with undeniable truth, my son was unfit to parent. We withdrew our petition and both parties walked away in silence. Later on and after much inner-reflection, I realized how selfish I had been. So much of this suffering seemed devastating for all of us, but I regret not supporting the baby's mother. I didn't have the right to put her through the stress and expense regardless of how I felt. Time may have resolved things differently and forcing the matter through the judicial system wouldn't change things.

As months passed my runaway child, Darinn, sunk deeper and deeper into the drug world. He literally became a homeless, soulless, heroin addict living in filth. In desperation, I searched for him. As his mother, my heart broke each time I spotted him on a street corner searching through garbage for soda cans. Dashing through traffic, I would park my car and race towards him before he vanished.

One unimaginable, stormy, dark night, I drove around for hours until I found him. Following him for a distance while still driving, I watched as he turned the corner into a deserted parking lot. When I ran from my car, afraid he had disappeared again, I found him incoherent, behind a dumpster, lying on a soiled mattress. That night, I begged. I cried. I sobbed my heart out pleading with him to enter a drug detox center. He refused. I don't know that he saw me standing in the rain or felt me pulling him by his arms. But my eyes were not blind to what was left of my son.

Seeing him skin and bones, not knowing what would happen to him was heart wrenching. Tears streaming, my heart aching, I turned to leave heavy with fear and guilt and a mother's pain. As I drove towards home a friend called. She is a therapist that understood how to help me disengage from a situation I could not control. Without her help, I'm not sure how I could have left without turning around.

Then in late 2005, Richard's contract was complete in northern Arizona so we returned to our home in Mexico. Lynsey was entering her senior year in high school and she came with us. Westin wanted to remain in Payson with a friend and his family to finish his junior year. Leaving was difficult for many reasons. Westin didn't want to be uprooted again and I didn't want to leave him behind. Financially, Richard would need to reestablish his business, and I knew life was going to abruptly change for me as well!

No matter where I lived, my need to help Darinn never changed. I continued searching for him once I left Payson. It's a six hour drive between my home and Tucson, Arizona and I would go often. Each attempt to reach out to him failed for several years, but one evening he called home and said he was ready to get help. He agreed to enter a drug rehabilitation center close to us.

Justin lives in Tucson. He returned in 2002 after he left Mexico and established a life there. He still works for the same company today and has a beautiful five year old daughter, Aly. She just started Kindergarten this year. He has faced his own bumps in the road but stays focused on his family and steadily employed.

After graduating from high school in Mexico in 2004, Nathan attended college in El Paso, Texas and then transferred to Mesa Community College in Arizona where he studied and also worked part-time for several years.

In 2006, Lynsey graduated from high school and after summer was over she left to enroll in a junior college in Tucson. But it is from the changes in her life during that time that radically changed our lives.

Westin returned home that fall for his senior year. How wonderful it was to spend time with him and enjoy the normalcy of a home life with a teen-ager. It was peaceful, and he was enthusiastic about life, friends, and music. I enjoyed having his friends over and our long, deep, heart-to-heart talks. He looked forward to his future. He has always been wise beyond his years and so often said, "I've learned and grown from what I've experienced around me."

My daughter and I are inseparable so when she left home, I said, "You aren't leaving here without me." How little did we know that would really come true? Her life was tumultuous for a time – frightening would better explain it. She became involved with a guy she cared for but I didn't feel good about the relationship from the beginning. As some girls do, she would tell me the good and hold back the truth.

She was a full time student and working part time. Her goal was to become a nurse, and she has the ability to be successful and the talent for limitless possibilities beyond her career. I wanted her to see herself as I do. Beautiful on the outside, compassionate on the inside and she deserves to be loved. But her relationship wasn't a healthy one and Lynsey was struggling. They would break up just to make up and soon she called me to say she was engaged.

This was one of my worst nightmares. My daughter was not to follow in my footsteps. First, I went through the emotional aspect of reliving my past and fearing the worst for her. But I learned something important from her experience and that was how to help her end it. She had to acknowledge the reality of the abuse in her relationship. She also had to own her feelings to feel her own her pain. It is difficult separating your true self and true feelings from co-dependent behaviors that include low self esteem and distorted boundaries. But when she opened up and talked about how she really felt, we were able to communicate, which gave me the opportunity to give her guidance and more awareness about herself. From my own background, I realize how force never works but how important intervention is. She needed my support *no matter what* and *no matter how many times* she broke up only to make up; I wasn't going to give up. It takes courage to walk away when you're not sure of yourself or if anyone else will love you. But the moment she said she was done, I was at her doorstep. We packed her belongings and together our strength was enough. This time she broke off her engagement for good and by early spring, 2007, she closed that chapter in her life,

A new chapter was beginning for Lynsey, but this time she was pregnant. Richard was living and working in El Paso, Texas. I was still in Mexico with Westin. Once he graduated in June of 2007, he stayed home until he left in December to serve a full time mission for the Mormon Church.

Since Lynsey needed to be away from her ex-boyfriend, and staying with me in the Mormon Community in Mexico really wasn't an option, she spent the next difficult nine months in Colorado Springs, CO.

To help Richard with his business, Nathan moved to El Paso and the two became partners. Rob left Tucson to also work with them. In time, he decided he really wanted to compete as a body builder, which led him to become a certified fitness trainer.

Darinn left the drug rehab in Mexico without completing the program. He found work in El Paso but was still drifting. Then he tried working for Richard but either drugs or alcohol continued to interfere with his life. Then at some point he was picked up by police for drug paraphernalia, later it was for failing to appear in court.

It became a cycle for him, in jail then out on probation. At times he was court mandated into drug facilities or half way houses but one day he began crossing the US border into Cd. Juarez, Mexico. Once again, he was using heroin. He would return for a few days and call home but one day the calls stopped coming.

Lynsey was struggling to get through her pregnancy. It was hard on her, a teen mom without the support she needed. She was basically alone, at least away from her immediate family and it was very difficult for me to be far away from her. I wanted her to be home. Yet, I also felt if she could work through this situation, she would find unknown strength and courage to face any storm.

The one I was the least worried about was Westin. My straight arrow always a shinning light never caused me to worry about him. But this also meant he received less nurturing and motherly influence, which was unfair. He deserved equal time and attention. It was difficult balancing the needs of each one when they were mostly in crisis. We talk about it today, and I'm grateful how well he has done. None-the-less, I'm not any less proud of the others as I am proud of him!

But it is the one, my "runaway child," that drew the most emotional energy from me that also went to a place in my heart I sealed. From so many dark nights of leaving him in the rain, and finding him on soiled mattresses with needless all around him, going with him to drug rehabilitation centers with high hopes only to have them dashed that finally the hurt went too deep.

Until one very cold winter night, I was at home alone. Worried again for children I couldn't take under my wings. Prayer has always been my retreat. There is peace for me in prayer and so I covered my body with the warmth of a quilt. Sitting close to the fire, I asked God to open my heart to the one who need me most at that moment, and in spirit, I would go to that child.

When I sat quietly with no thought of my own, tears quickly sprang, and I wept. I said, "No, not this child, God. If I open my heart, I will open to the pain." But it wasn't pain that I felt it was dread. All night I stayed with Darinn in soul and spirit and took him into my heart. I felt death. I wasn't sure if he was clinging to life or if his spirit had already left his lifeless body but was still lingering. I begged him to go into the Light and not to be afraid, but if he was still living, I begged God to help us get to him.

The next morning, I called Richard and told him what happened the night before. He didn't hesitate when I said, "you need to find Darinn now." Rob and Nathan got together and crossed over the border into one of the worst drug infested areas looking for him. This was just before the drug wars broke out and turned Cd. Juarez, Mexico into a horrific bloodshed city. I was afraid for their safety going into an area where crime and killings had already taken place out in the open frequently. It took them nearly a week of crossing the border daily until one day Richard went with them and everything fell into place.

They met a man on a street corner that knew someone with information regarding Darinn. My son stands out. He is tall and blonde and extremely friendly. He knows everyone no matter where he goes and this time they were taken to where he stayed. Had they not found him more than likely he wouldn't be here today. Darinn had over-dosed on heroin nearly a week before and a friend he was with thought he was dead. He was ready to dump his body into a canal where most victims go but Darinn pulled through. Richard and his two brothers were able to convince him to return, face the consequences of parole violation, and try to fix his life,

Lynsey gave birth to Caelyn on October 15th 2007. I wasn't there for her birth. She came earlier than expected. I had to drive three hours to the airport and then catch a flight to Colorado Springs. The moment this little girl was placed in my arms, I knew she was all mine for a little while. The love I felt emanating from her heart was heavenly. God sent her with an old soul in a tiny little body, whose heart is more loving than any I've ever felt. This child is like magic and she still believes in fairies, and unicorns with wings. When she grows up she wants to be a princess with a wand in her hand that has powers. At her tender little age, she has no idea the power she has or the magic she instills in every heart she touches.

Lynsey and I stayed at home for a few months after Caelyn was born. It was then obvious that I *really* was going to be Caelyn's primary caregiver. My daughter wasn't ready to be a mom, she was still so young. I also knew she was suffering from postpartum depression. But I didn't want to be Caelyn's mother. She needed to bond with her own mom and Lynsey just needed time to finish growing up and do some healing work herself.

Any thoughts of having my own career vanished the moment Lynsey told me she was pregnant. It didn't take a fortune teller to tell me she wasn't ready to be a mother, but we both knew from the beginning this baby was meant to be!

Caelyn's welfare was my highest priority and keeping her together with her mother was part of that so all three of us moved to Mesa, Arizona. Lynsey needed to move forward with her life and she couldn't do it sitting at home in Mexico without any existing opportunities. As tough as it was living together, loving and caring for Caelyn for the next 17 months would change my life in ways never imagined.

Lynsey and I worked through some pretty tough issues. She was angry with me. She felt abandoned during the years I was severely depressed and sick. Growing up without her mother to guide and protect her left many scars. Often she took that out on me and it was painful. I didn't know what else to do other than take responsibility when appropriate and learn to be strong and communicate openly with true feelings. What became the healing force between us, and has carried us forward into an extraordinary mother and daughter relationship is Caelyn. Our love for Caelyn and sharing the gift of raising her together was the beginning of healing our past.

While Lynsey worked full time, I cared for this beautiful baby with heart and soul. We were inseparable. For the first time, I knew what it felt like to simply love a baby. Together we entered into her world of lullabies and butterflies. Everything was beautiful. Every song that played, we sang along. We made numerous road trips together. Each trip from Arizona to Texas and across the border to Mexico was eventful – oh how I loved this child with big brown eyes and the chubbiest, rosy checks – she was my little cherub!

Finally, I felt it was time to leave Mesa and take Caelyn with me. As soon as Lynsey was ready, she also left to relocate in El Paso and to be closer to family.

Richard, Rob and Nate already had a home in El Paso so I stayed there with Caelyn until Lynsey arrived. My, oh my, was this the 4th of July or just an explosion of fireworks between Nathan, Rob and Lynsey? Obviously, it was between the three of them and I didn't want any part of it. There must have been unfinished business for me too because every time I tried to leave something happened to prevent it.

This wasn't the way Nathan planned it and he wasn't the least bit happy. He called Justin one day and said, "Hey, bro, why not join us? The rest of the family is here." Well, not everyone was living together. Westin was still on his mission and the judge decided Darinn needed to do a little jail time! And my bags were packed! I was ready to head south of the border as soon as fate allowed me to go. It was frustrating having to depend on someone else to make that happen. Either it was car repairs or work related but I was so ready to go after weeks turned into months.

One day after listening to enough arguments over petty things, I marched through a door I just ran out of and hollered at everyone to sit down! This time they did as they were told. Three grown kids looked bewildered as if something was missing on my face. Nothing was missing! In fact; something emerged! Courage. I wasn't going to take Caelyn and run from these war-waging, three year-olds. They were going to learn a tough, life lesson for as long as it took to return their hearts to love. At that point, I had no doubt of a "Higher" source drawing each of us together while guiding us on this unexpected journey – one that I relied immensely on the still small voice for guidance.

We had a long talk that afternoon. Lecturing as any frustrated mom would do, I let them know that as soon as they learned to get along they wouldn't all be living at home with daddy. You just have to know Richard to know he is the salt of the earth. He was up to the task of bearing through this transformational stage but it was also for his own highest good.

It was difficult for these three adult siblings to live together under the same roof. From the inside it seemed to be the worst idea ever, but had they lived a part the wounds they carried would still remain. It's sort of like putting them inside a tea pot, closing the lid, and melting their difficult, exterior personalities. Then once added together with the right ingredients, boiling the water until it became quite like the little tempest pot, they learned to grow beyond the anger and love through the pain.

The love Lynsey's brother's feel for this little girl gave them a cause to stay and work together in support of their sister and a precious baby they fiercely protect. Otherwise, they would have thrown up their hands or throttled someone with them or fled the country like I did.

Long ago, I learned how painful it can be to swim upstream rather than flow with the stream and that's what I wanted them to understand. Some how they needed to know, "No one is going to escape from the tea pot until they lift the lid with love." Once my kids came together for a common cause, I knew God would work through them and how could they not be changed by love?

Fast-forward: Today, Nathan is single and dating. He is also a business partner with Richard.

Rob is a certified fitness trainer, married to Gulyhan; they have Brian, (5) and Skyler, (2 months.)

Lynsey is married to Matt; they have Camry, (11) Caelyn, (5) Chloe, (1). Lynsey is close to her BA in Social Work and is sworn in as an Advocate for Children in El Paso, Texas.

Justin remains in Tucson, Arizona, with Aly, (5) and they visit our family in El Paso every holiday. I see them as often as I can while traveling in-between the two states.

Westin is a college student in Mesa, Arizona. He is working towards an engineering degree, working part time, and enjoying life. I miss being around him. He is a deep thinker and I learn so much from him.

Darinn has been the most difficult one to write about. When I came to this part of the book, the life he lives and the painful past surfaced. The sealed portion of my heart wasn't tight enough. The problem with writing a memoir such as this is the integrity in doing so. What parts do I leave out? Do I have to spill all of our family secrets? For years, Darinn was out there somewhere. If I didn't feel him as being part of me, and our family, getting through the problems in front of me was all I could bear. Now I can't. He is here. I've made him real again. The truth is he has six more months to go before he is released from prison.

Had he been able to (or chosen) to remain drug or alcohol free and completed his probation terms he wouldn't be where he is today. Each chance he had, he gave up and he is out of chances. It would be easier to use the delete key and erase the parts I don't want to face or for others to read, but I won't. These are all cold facts of the reality of battered women and abused children. Nothing I have written is excuses. We are each responsible for our happiness and how we chose to deal with our experiences. I'm not a licensed therapist, so I'm not giving advice. I only write from experience and from mistakes I've made, but if it saves one from going down this path then how great is my joy.

23

When Dreams Fall Through

When you least expect it your Spirit awakens and softly whispers...
"When dreams fall through have courage to live true to your
own destiny. Steer the course and you will know your calling.

Over the years, the colors of my life seemed to fade away as each season passed before me. Who am I? I asked the wind one day. A melody, rustling leaves beneath my feet and bending flower heads silently rushed by me, but nothing would answer me.

Sun-dappled memories of a child are still calling out to me. Longing to grasp her tiny hand and bring her safely home takes my breath away. Distantly, her eyes fade in morning light, and my eyes begin to see. Her golden hair of honey melts against my face, mysteriously reminding me, she isn't gone she's still here with me.

Years have passed and vanished into thin air, and although I'm certainly no longer a child, I hold to her fallen-dreams. I'm a grown woman who has felt her share of pain. Yet, is it possible to integrate this little girl with all her wonder into the woman I am becoming?

Victimized for many years, I felt less than other people. My pain, a silent scream of despair begged for release——disquiet between heart and soul grew in strength and intensity, until it became a roaring rage. With blatant expression of grief, the silencing of my heart returned with misery, and the only thing standing between my broken heart and wholeness was *truth*.

As real as it gets, I journeyed through disappointments, heartache and anguish until my heart felt nothing but betrayal. An emotional breakdown finally became the break through that I needed. Only then was I forced to let go of a life that wasn't mine and believe in the one that is.

Once I found it, I gave it all I had. When I had to let go of having it my way, and of expecting this dream to unfold in my time, I faced another long winter without spring and my fallen dream felt like death and decay. Perhaps it was too much grief over a span of a lifetime or too many losses.

I'm not sure what brought me to the edge of life, but I know when I first began weaving myself inside the "proverbial" butterfly cocoon; I felt nothing except a deep need to feel something. Tiny pieces of me washed away revealed an emptiness that had gone unattended. Once my children were no longer at home, I felt alone inside an empty nest.

Richard and I spent most of our time as fire fighters. There was always a crisis to face, a child to save, but what really put the fire out in me happened when I lost sight of my own dreams. I also realized something else was missing – an emotional connection to my husband. Somehow, perhaps over time, we didn't grow together as much as we grew apart. I felt alone as if we stood on separate sides of an island.

In spite of the passing years, and all the wisdom experience has instilled in me, I still want to paint my world with living color, restore shattered dreams, and feel deeply loved and cherished. I want to walk along a deserted beach in windblown skirts and sun-kissed shoulders; I want to see the beauty as I age gracefully.

I want to be strong enough to stop taking the blame, and feeling a rush of panic when things fall apart, and I can't repair the damage. I want to live my life in peace and not seen as a victim – someone who has required great sacrifice to care for. I want to hear singing birds, and feel rapture in each breath I take; I want to know I matter.

I certainly don't want to leave this Earth a troubled woman filled with remorse and regret for not fulfilling my life calling. It certainly isn't enough to heal broken wings and not use them or to silence the storms and not joyfully sing with all women.

I've come to realize how important it is to be self-contained and to hold strong to our dreams so this path unfolds. There is a voice within each of us to guide us on this journey allowing the seed of perfection to unfold. Within this seed is a pattern for our individual lives. A pattern, which if allowed to blossom with nurturance and attendance to our inner voice will unfold. No one knows of our path – they can't tell us what it is or what we will experience as we journey.

I had no idea what to expect, but my heart seemed to draw me back to Arizona in 2010. If I tried explaining all that happened or the rationality of it, I would have to write another book! There are so many things I'm not so proud of, but there is a reason for each important step I experienced. Part of that included filing for divorce. It felt like everything in my past was coming to a close, and I had to let go of whatever it was that prevented me from living authentically – true to my Inner Self – a way in which would allow new life to begin.

Sometimes growth can be painful, it isn't always easy. At least it has been this way for me. This process of change is a cycle, which is similar to that of the caterpillar dying to the butterfly. The ending of a cycle is a time to get rid of old beliefs, self doubt and fear that doesn't support us. Change may be small or significant, but I've learned to still my heart and listen. It is where I find guidance and comfort. Opportunities were given to me to grow beyond the limitations that held me back, and this was challenging.

Indeed, I can say, throughout out this unique journey, I was deeply troubled as the answers I needed often eluded me. At times, I felt like I was going in circles. Then I stopped long enough to watch soft breezes gently kiss the vines clinging to the arbor outside my window. Moved by silent touch, they remain the same today as yesterday and the year before, yet, am I?

This overflowing fragrant vine, filled with blooming honeysuckle, permeates the air with an enchanting scent uniquely its own. It also wraps itself around everything else in sight.

I can't untangle its limbs and tiny tendrils to separate one from another. Is it this way for me? Am I so afraid of change; I cling to the past? Am I still so entangled in the lives of those I love; I've stopped living my life? Are the opinions and beliefs of others still more important than my own?

My pain as a battered woman fades in comparison to my grief as a mother. Distraught and discouraged, I wanted to lay this aging woman to rest; it seemed the right thing to do. She had paid penance for all her wrong doings. Then I realized that I *was* moving forward. I had given up enough of me and it was time to nurture my needs and establish a life of my own. This is the only way to become self-contained and overcome fear. We find a sense of inner balance and peace on our way to self mastery. Each step we take draws us deeper into a well of Light and Love until we become Love and Light. It isn't something we are given or something we can give, but we can teach others to find the well once we find our way.

Deep in thought, I feel the currents and whispering winds telling me I am above the valley and beyond that place of strife and to live my life in peace. High into the mountaintops and across the azure sky, I'm soaring groundless and free. I've found my way living each moment as it unfolds. Ending each night with prayer knowing God is within. I'm also reminded daily of the times God gave me signs – yes, go forward – you are on your path.

The emergence of the butterfly from the cocoon state is also symbolic of our spiritual awakening out of the "self-imposed" limitations of the physical world. All that has gone before, which is our own personal past, strengthens our wings. As for the butterfly, her own transformation is total. While in her cocoon state, she is completely still. After she emerges, she is strengthened by her struggle and has wings to fly. When we overcome fear and doubt, we are also strengthened by our struggle. Fear has no real objective except to act as a warning and to propel us forward.

If we learn to hold our minds in a symphony of praise and glory, we also learn how important it is to dance when it is raining, and to sing when we are afraid. In doing so it is through our trials we are humbled to reach deep into the recesses of our sacred minds and heart's for guidance and comfort.

One of my most difficult challenges came after a long absence from family and from challenges that broke my heart open to an ache deeper than I ever felt. Someone came into my life that awakened my spirit. Our connection was purely on a soul level, but he ignited a deep love flowing through my veins pulsating into my heart. I lived in Arizona while he was living in a different state but he couldn't have felt closer.

Someday, I will fully understand the purpose of our paths crossing, but not just yet. I feel he will find me on the other side, but for now softly he whispers how grateful he is fate brought me to him. I waited for him to be well again. Believing with all my heart, God would let him live after learning he had cancer three months after we met. He made it through treatment, but his heart was damaged. Ten months later, in April of 2010, he crossed over to the other side.

My heart was damaged too. I was inconsolable and this time the weight was too heavy. I'm not sure how to explain the next ten months, but I entered into aspects of me that are inexplicable except to say it felt dark as if I was in my own personal hell. I didn't stay in this place, but I passed through it. I also returned to be with my family in El Paso just before Thanksgiving. Although Richard and I are divorced, he is still tightly knitted into my family and he was supportive.

The holidays were bleak. Lynsey was pregnant with Chloe, and she needed my emotional support. I stayed with her through Thanksgiving and Christmas, but returned to my home in Mexico in January. Her birthday is on the 28th of February, so friends of hers helped me plan a baby shower and a birthday party on the same day. That would give me time to be alone and in my own familiar surroundings for a while, so I thought, "Ok, you can do this. This is something to look forward to, something to awaken your spirit."

But I wasn't feeling like celebrating. I wanted to stay home where I could crawl into my own bed and just sleep forever. So when I'm at my lowest point, when I have no will to go on, I feel the same sensation – a whispering Voice telling me, "it's time to go," and I say, "oh, no! I'm not going anywhere."

Its early morning and I'm still in my pajamas. The air is brisk and cold enough for a fire to be burning in the fireplace on February 22, 2011. I'm in my kitchen pacing the floor talking to myself. It really was an argument because I wasn't going anywhere and, no, I wasn't having another breakdown. But I was near throwing a tantrum if forced to pack a suitcase, get in my car, and drive to El Paso just because I was telling myself to go. This time, I was through listening to voices no matter where they came from but by noon the feeling inside was building. "Ok," I thought, "this isn't going away, so do I go or do I stay?" Then I felt the words as though they were spoken out loud, "and you would deny me now?"

As I'm throwing clothes in the back seat of my black Tahoe, I'm thinking, there better be a solid, clear reason for this or else I will know for sure… I've really lost my mind! I arrived late that evening and stayed with Lynsey. The next morning, she leaves her apartment, drops off Caelyn at daycare, and heads for campus. I call Rob and tell him to meet me at the gym. I didn't stay very long. Something didn't feel right. When I drove home something wasn't right. If I turned left, I went right. When I tried using my cell phone, my fingers didn't function. Finally, by chance, I dialed my friend, Patsy, but my words didn't come out right.

Focusing really hard to make sure I stayed in one lane, I had to make two left turns to reach Lynsey's apartment. By then it was more difficult to function. Once inside, I was shutting down like someone disconnected all the wires to my brain. That didn't alarm me though, I thought lying down would fix everything. What choice did I have? I couldn't turn the knob to the front door so I wasn't going anywhere. Unable to use my cell phone at all there was no one to call.

Lynsey came home early from her classes because she felt something wasn't right. She didn't stop to pick up Caelyn instead she came straight home. When she saw me and tried talking to me, she said, "mom, get your shoes on. I'm taking you to the hospital."

Once inside the ER, I just remember feeling confused, weak, and babbling and then seizures. Nurses and doctors were coming in and out of the room. My sons had arrived and I saw panic on their faces. Lynsey's eyes were red. She tried not to let me see but she broke down and left the room. Then I was afraid. She was my voice. No one else understood a word I said, but I felt Lynsey could read my mind, and she would tell them for me, "Don't let me die."

Later that evening I was in ICU. The following morning was the first time I remember knowing I had a large tumor on the left side of my brain. Surgery was scheduled for the following morning.

Humbled beyond words, silently I whispered a prayer of gratitude. I, who doubt first and must have proof before I believe, would not have life except for the Still Small Voice. At the edge of this precious breath of Energy that sustains us, I was also at the edge without a will to go on. This was a moment of Truth magnified by the love that surrounded me. What did I really want? Maybe the answers I wanted regarding my past didn't really matter. What mattered was in front me – my children and this present moment in which I still had life.

Surgery took six hours. My neurosurgeon removed a Meningioma Tumor, which is generally a benign tumor that slowing grows in the meninges or the membranes surrounding the brain. Not knowing I had this tumor, it must have shifted or had a sudden growth spurt but it became life threatening. Had I not listened to the warning Voice I felt a few days before; I wouldn't have had medical intervention in time.

My family came together drawing from each other's strength to give me more than enough. Never have I felt so loved, and, yet, so undeserving at the same time. There is a hymn, one of my favorites and just one line says everything for me, "because I have been given much I too must give."

In return, quietly my heart sings a melody to a woman's long forgotten song. From years of heartache, pain taught me compassion and tender mercy. Loneliness taught me to stop looking for someone to love me and find it in my own heart. In search of answers, doors opened each time I knocked. Every step I took in search of little girl lost brought me to a deep place of Self awareness where I learned to quiet the inner critic and find less fault in others. How can I not breathe appreciation for all these poignant insights that taught me *beyond mortal experience* is life eternal where hope springs from?

I would like to share this sacred experience with you, so you can also know that in all conditions there is always hope. You must know that from the heartbreak in your life there are blessings found in courage. Sometimes we think we want mountains to move when all that we really want is the courage to face the challenge and the strength to climb to the top. There is a different view from the heights we achieve, a perspective we can't see from the bottom and a heart that never beats the same. As we journey into the depths of our inner Self, on our way we find our calling and true meaning to life.

Prayer and meditation grounds and centers me especially during times of fear. It brings me comfort to find my center and on one particular night; I wanted reassurance that I was moving forward taking the right steps. For several years, I felt I would help many women heal from abuse, but I was discouraged and doubted in my abilities. So I asked for the Spirit's help.

Drawing from the power of meditation, I visualized light surrounding my body and as the light grew stronger, I felt myself leave this Earth plane and go deeper within feeling a Love all-powerful and glorious fill my being.

Breathtakingly, my prayer was answered as light entered my darkened room. I could see silvery outlines of spiritual beings in radiant and shimmering light.

Then, I saw a misty doorway opening as an even more beautiful light came closer. The light was so radiant and the love so pure, I could scarcely breathe. I wept in awe at the glory of this being.

As she drew closer, I knew she was another dimension to my spirit. I could not deny her presence as she held out her hand.

Silent words filled my heart and I began to speak the words out loud for her: *"You are a Creator Goddess and have chosen to be here during these most difficult times to help bring healing to this Earth. You knew the knowledge you would need could only come from personal suffering.*

My life passed before me, with a review of all I had experienced.

The memory of a woman's face and her worthlessness filled my heart with sorrow. I wept knowing this was not who I was, and at that moment, I also realized even Christ suffered to feel our pain.

Beyond anything we could dream of, God knows our hearts and what we can achieve, and beyond sorrow, fear, and defeat, *hope survives*. We need to believe in the Light within – the power that exists in every human soul to receive all the goodness in life, and to achieve wholeness and unity with God. We need to believe that beyond the ignorance of mankind is a Loving Force guiding us and this planet towards light and peace. This is the Spirit of Truth, Eternal Life and Light and Love. As we begin to rely upon our own intuition, the Light Within, seek this comfort, and believe in the power to create lives of greater joy, our lives will unfold and take form through Divine Will – this is not beyond our reach; it is our birthright.

Because of this, I'm grateful for the whimsical memories of the child I used to be as she danced upon her stage with music sweeping her into a world of fantasy. From all that has gone before a joyous melody plays as I believe in hope, faith and love. Knowing that beyond this world and a zillion stars someone watches over me, and that beyond my own vision, God see's a whole new world opening for me gives strength to my wings.

Yet, even the wings of the butterfly must dry before she flies. Her journey isn't over once she frees herself from the cocoon. Patiently, we must also wait, learning to stay focused in the present, but if we stay true to the eternal principles of life, our wings will unfold beautiful and strong.

Even though yellow faded photographs, timeless in memory, reflect this woman shaped by many voices and experiences, never once did Truth fade away. She only grew wiser beyond her own knowing with courage and strength because of *the power of God's Love.*

Resources

* ***Tough love*** is an approach in which you ***do not enable*** a child to wreck havoc in the home. Enduring life with a troubled teen that is running the home can result in many battles and arguments and sometimes physical and verbal abuse. Tough love is exactly that: **tough**. Loving our children is unconditional, but we don't have to like what they are doing or how they are destroying their lives. *You can literally love your child to death and do more harm when you enable or allow behavior that is unhealthy.*

There may come a time when you say ***enough is enough***! This is the time you need support from outside sources, such as parent support groups or a local therapist.

Many times tough love is simply letting go. You may need to let your teen-ager make his or her own mistake and learn from their consequences.

It is vital that you, as parent(s) and other family members also get healthy. Recovery is a family matter. Each of you need help and support. There are groups such as "Nar-Anon, and "Al-Anon Family Groups," in your community when your child is also abusing drugs and/or alcohol.

I would encourage you to seek professional counseling and find "Tough Love Support Groups," in your area. There is no shame nor should you feel guilty as a parent when you have problems within your family. Most important is that you get the help you need.

Websites for information:

- http://www.Violence Resources @ Child Net
- http://www.Parenting Teens.com
- http://Juvenile Programs Resources.com
- http://Youth & Children Net Parents Index
- http://Teen-Anon

A Book I also highly recommend is, Co-dependent No More, by: Melody Beattie.

There are many good websites relating to codependency, which refers to unhealthy behavior. Research these websites and go to your local bookstore in the Self Help section to find books relating to your specific needs.

Domestic Violence: Call your local crisis shelter for support and counseling. If you are in danger call 911. Don't wait. Get the help you need for your self and your children. For Teen Dating Violence: http://nomoreabuse.com

http://thehotline.org

http://domesticviolence.org